S0-BRD-593

AUTISM
TREATMENT
GUIDE

Elizabeth K. Gerlach

Four Leaf Press
Eugene, Oregon

IMPORTANT:

This book is for informational purposes only; the author does not endorse any treatments described. Before beginning a new treatment for yourself or your child, consult a physician. The author disclaims any liability arising directly or indirectly from the use of the book.

Copyright © 1993, Revised 1998 by Elizabeth K. Gerlach. All rights reserved.

First Edition.

Fourteenth Printing, January 1999

The author is grateful for permission to reprint the following copyrighted material:

Excerpt from the *Diagnostic and Statistical Manual of Mental Disorders, Fourth Edition*, copyright © 1994. Used by permission of the American Psychiatric Association.

Excerpt from *Food Makes the Difference*, copyright ©1985 by Patricia McEntire-Kane, PhD. Used by permission of Simon & Schuster, Inc.

Excerpt from "Autism: Basic Information." Used by permission of the New Jersey Center for Outreach Services.

"Definition of Autism" used by permission of the Autism Society of America.

Library of Congress Catalog Card Number 93-91648

ISBN-0-9637578-0-6

Designed by Graphics Unlimited

Cover design: Ken Austin
Published by: Four Leaf Press
P.O. Box 23502
Eugene, Oregon 97402

Printed in the United States of America

TABLE OF CONTENTS

FOREWORD

Parents of autistic children owe an immense debt of gratitude to Elizabeth Gerlach. This little guidebook will not only save them countless hours of searching out resources, but will also help assure them that they will not overlook any of the major treatment options that are "out there" for them to consider.

This guidebook has been needed for a very long time, and will be eagerly welcomed by parents and professionals alike.

Good work, Elizabeth, and *thank you*!

Bernard Rimland, PhD., Director
Autism Research Institute

ACKNOWLEDGMENTS

Without the help and support of many wonderful people, this book would have remained only an idea. I would like to thank Jane Novick, not only for her editing expertise, but also for opening her heart and home to my whole family and for being a most wonderful friend.

I also wish to thank Dr. Stephen Edelson, Director of the Center for the Study of Autism, for reviewing this work, and encouraging and supporting me in this endeavor.

Thanks to The Autism Society of America and the Autism Research Institute for helping parents like me understand autism, and for providing us with the information and support we need to help our children with autism.

Also my gratitude to Jane and Ken Austin, Leslie King, Clayton King, and F.E. McNeil for technical assistance, art-work, and support, and to Joan Cookson for assistance with the printing. Thanks to all the many professionals (Svea Gold, Rob O'Neill, Dr. Skye Weintraub, Kathleen Hogan, Kelly Oatman, Gita Wertz, and Carol Lee Berger) who read the material for accuracy of content; Valda Fields for the vote of confidence. Thanks to Patricia Marucci for her willingness to lend an ear or a hug, and to Janine Fisher, for her inspiring energy and effort.

Many thanks to Rand, for his support of my writing and his devotion to our family. Finally, special thanks to my children, who are my greatest teachers.

AUTHOR'S NOTE

As a parent of a child diagnosed with autism, I have talked with parents, gone to workshops, picked the library clean, and I still keep my eyes and ears open for ways to help my son. But what I've needed all along is a book that has information on treatments in one accessible place. I needed it to know what was available to help my son when he was first diagnosed. I wasted a lot of "early intervention" time by being unaware of treatment options. While certain treatments may be more effective if our children are younger, our quest for helping them is a life-long endeavor. To do this, we must be aware of the possibilities. I've found the adage, "knowledge is power," a motto to live by as I raise my child with special needs.

I am an optimist and a realist. I know there are no "miracle cures" for autism. Yet, I am not afraid to dream of the day when there might be. I can still hold on to that dream even if it is with the nail on my little finger.

What I don't like is people telling me what I should or shouldn't try as a means to help my child. Therefore, this book offers only straightforward information and *does not endorse any treatment*. If you are a parent, I respect you as the expert on your child, and I trust you to choose the treatments that are right for your child. If you are a professional, I urge you to respect a parent's judgment, even if you disagree, and to be as supportive as you can. Please don't blame us parents for trying, for hoping.

Regarding treatments for autism, what works wonders for one individual may have absolutely no effect on another. I wish I could say, "This really helped my son, maybe you should try it," but that would be setting a lot of you up for disappointment. What makes a successful treatment? To me, a successful treatment improves the quality of my son's life or my family's life, often in small but significant ways. Say we try a particular treatment, and my son sleeps through the night for the first time in his life, but he still wakes up autistic. I say that treatment is a success; if we are well rested everyone benefits. But what if I try a method that takes time and patience to follow through, but ultimately I see no results? I give myself credit for trying to help and I move on without regrets.

I think it is important for people to realize that treatments can and should be combined. For instance, experts warn that medications should not be given as a substitute for a consistent behavior management program. Likewise, sensory integration therapy could be incorporated into a child's school day if it helps him or her handle stressful situations. While I think it is important for purposes of research to know what treatments make a noticeable difference, once this has been established why not combine them as you try to improve the quality of your life or the life of your child.

I realize that information is constantly changing. As soon as this book is printed someone will have changed a phone number or a zip code. Yet I hope it can be of help to you. I don't claim to have included every treatment that could help someone with autism. I know that having kids with autism swim with dolphins shows promise, but the closest most of us can get to that one is renting *Flipper* at the video store. Now there's an idea . . .

Elizabeth Gerlach
Eugene, Oregon

Autism Defined

For years, children with autism were thought to have emotional problems or to suffer from schizophrenia. We now know that this is not true. Autism is a physical disorder characterized by specific symptoms that vary in kind and severity with each individual. **The following definition of autism is reprinted here from the Autism Society of America.**

AUTISM is a severely incapacitating life-long developmental disability that typically appears during the first three years of life. The result of a neurological disorder that affects functioning of the brain, autism and its behavioral symptoms occur in approximately fifteen out of every 10,000 births. Autism is four times more common in boys than girls. It has been found throughout the world in families of all racial, ethnic, and social backgrounds. No known factors in the psychological environment of a child have been shown to cause autism.

Some behavioral symptoms of autism include:

(1) Disturbances in the rate of appearance of physical, social, and language skills.

(2) Abnormal responses to sensations. Any one or a combination of senses or responses are affected: sight, hearing, touch, balance, smell, taste, reaction to pain, and the way a child holds his or her body.

(3) Speech and language are absent or delayed, while specific thinking capabilities may be present.

(4) Abnormal ways of relating to people, objects, and events.

Autism occurs by itself or in association with other disorders which affect the function of the brain such as viral infections, metabolic disturbances, and epilepsy. It is important to distinguish autism from retardation or mental disorders since diagnostic confusion may result in referral to inappropriate and ineffective treatment techniques. The severe form of the syndrome may include extreme self-injurious, repetitive, highly unusual, and aggressive behavior. Special education programs using behavioral methods have proved to be the most helpful treatment for persons with autism.

AUTISM IS TREATABLE…Early diagnosis and intervention are vital to the future development of the child. [Reprinted with permission from the Autism Society of America.]

Diagnosis

Autism is a confusing disorder because it presents itself in unique ways in each affected individual. Some children with autism may show severe cognitive impairment, whereas others may show incredible skills in math, memory, or art, but are severely lacking in social skills. Some individuals cannot speak, whereas others are verbal, although their speech may lack meaning to those around them. Many individuals with autism insist on sameness in their environment, exhibit repetitive behaviors such as rocking, engage in routinized, unimaginative play, and seem to be aloof or unaware of their environment and the people in it.

Dr. Leo Kanner was one of the first professionals in the field of psychiatry to identify children who exhibited autistic characteristics as a separate group from those labeled schizophrenic. Yet it has taken decades for professionals to recognize and understand the nature of autism. Dr. Bernard Rimland's book, *Infantile Autism: The Syndrome and Its*

Implications for a Neural Theory of Behavior, published in 1964, broke ground in the area of autism. It debunked the assumption that autism was a result of "bad" parenting, and it helped to establish autism as a neurobiological disorder.

Although the degrees of severity vary greatly from individual to individual, one common thread among those with autism is the impairment of communication skills in a social context. Lack of eye contact, rigid or concrete thinking, difficulty in processing information, sensory problems, anxiety, and echolalic speech are just a few of the factors that may interfere with an individual's ability to create reciprocal social interactions.

Autism is behaviorally defined. There are no medical tests that can be administered to establish a diagnosis of autism, although tests can rule out or identify other underlying problems. In order to determine a diagnosis of autism, professionals depend on observation of the behavioral characteristics of each individual. Basically, the more autistic behaviors a person exhibits, the more likely it is that they will be diagnosed as having autism.

Obtaining a correct diagnosis can be a major hurdle. Most experts in the field of autism would agree that an evaluation conducted by an interdisciplinary team is the ideal choice when autism is suspected. Such an evaluation team consists of professionals from a variety of specialty areas working together to determine a diagnosis. The team may include, but is not limited to, a psychologist, a pediatrician with knowledge of autism, an educational diagnostician, a speech/language pathologist, an audiologist, and perhaps a social worker. Parents play a critical role in the process of diagnosis by providing information on the child's developmental history and behaviors. Because autism is a behaviorally defined disorder, it stands to reason that the more professionals who observe the behaviors at various times and in various settings, the better the chance of making an accurate diagnosis of autism; it is certainly better than having one specialist evaluate alone.

To determine a child's disorder, professionals must also determine what disorders are not present. The comparison of the behaviors of the child being diagnosed with behaviors typically seen in other disorders is known as "differential diagnosis." Mental retardation and/or language disorder are two major disorders that must be investigated. The child is also tested for medical and genetic problems, such as Phenylketonuria (PKU) and Fragile-X Syndrome, which are sometimes seen in conjunction with autism. [See Powers, pp. 12-15.]

When evaluating a child with developmental problems, doctors and psychologists often use the American Psychiatric Association's Fourth Edition of the *Diagnostic and Statistical Manual of Mental Disorders* (DSMIV, 1994), which outlines criteria for identifying most disorders, both mental and emotional. Autism falls under the subclass, "Pervasive Developmental Disorders." For "Autistic Disorder," the DSMIV lists twelve diagnostic criteria falling into three major categories: impairment in social interaction, impairments in communication, and a restricted repertoire of activities and interests. The diagnosis of autism is made if the child displays at least six of the 12 symptoms and a minimum number in each category. Also, the onset of these symptoms must have occurred during infancy or early childhood.

Some individuals with autistic-like behaviors may not meet all the criteria for a diagnosis of "Autistic Disorder"; in this case, they are sometimes given the diagnosis, "Pervasive Developmental Disorder Not Otherwise Specified" (PDDNOS). Many researchers feel that the term "pervasive developmental disorder" is inaccurate and unfair. Individuals with autistic-like symptoms who are diagnosed with PDDNOS may not be given the legal rights of those with autism. Many professionals feel that autism is not a "pervasive" disorder, but one in which "specific" social/cognitive skills are impaired. It has been suggested that a new category be developed for determining the presence of autism. [See Baird, et al., pp. 363-64.] Meanwhile, professionals will continue to use the criteria set forth in the DSMIV, which is continually revised to reflect changes in criteria for various disorders.

Researchers are working to devise new ways of testing for autism in very young children. These tests may prove to be an extremely valuable tool because early intervention may make a significant difference in the treatment of individuals with autism. Such a test, developed by researchers Simon Baron-Cohen, Jane Allen, and Christopher Gillberg, is the "Checklist for Autism in Toddlers" (CHAT). Questions on this test regard social interactions, imaginative play, communication skills (verbal and nonverbal cues), and imitation. This 14-question test is given to parents and physicians familiar with the child. In the first controlled study, researchers tentatively identified four out of 91 children (all 18-months old) who were all later positively identified with autism at 30 months of age. [See Allen, pp. 839-43.] Follow-up studies are investigating the effectiveness of this test.

The Autism Research Institute distributes a diagnostic checklist, known as Form E-2, first published in 1964, which was designed primarily as a screening instrument to help researchers identify children with autism considered for participation in research studies. Also, Form E2 is designed to help in the process of diagnosing children who have been labeled autistic, autistic-like, schizophrenic, or

PDDNOS. Only five to ten percent of children labeled autistic fit the description of early infantile autism as defined by Leo Kanner in 1943. Parents or professionals complete the questionnaire, giving answers based on behaviors the child exhibited between the ages of three and five. The Institute scores the child on both behavior and speech patterns and combines these for a total score. The child is scored on a scale ranging from -45 to +45. Any score above +20 indicates a probable case of early infantile autism. Children who score from -15 to +19 are typically regarded as autistic by professionals. Children whose scores are -16 or lower are usually described as "autistic-like" (or labeled with some similar term). Scoring is done at no charge, and results are returned to the parents or professionals who submitted the form.

Sometimes, parents of a child with a disability must rely on an evaluation conducted by their school district. If parents have doubts or questions concerning the outcome of this evaluation, parents may seek further evaluations from outside the school system. If the results differ, the school district is legally responsible for payment of the private evaluation, unless it can prove at a due process hearing that the district's evaluation was appropriate. The school district must consider the results of a private evaluation when making decisions concerning the child.

There are other syndromes, such as Tourette Syndrome, Rett Syndrome, and Asperger Syndrome, in which characteristics of autism are often present. Asperger Syndrome is probably a form of high-functioning autism. Professionals are moving toward identifying subgroups of autism, and this will undoubtedly be a long and involved process. Little is known about the exact causes of the disorder, although research has uncovered brain abnormalities in some individuals with autism.

There is a movement among professionals to create a subclassification system for autism in order to better understand the differences between individuals. [See du Verglas, pp. 8-11.] Ongoing research may find possible genetic links, environmental factors, abnormalities in brain structure, and/or neurobiological factors that may contribute to autism and related disorders.

The American Psychiatric Association's *Diagnostic and Statistical Manual of Mental Disorders* (Fourth Edition) lists these criteria for **299.00 Autistic Disorder:**

A. A total of six (or more) items from (1), (2), and (3), with at least two from (1), and one each from (2) and (3):

(1) qualitative impairment in social interaction, as manifested by at least two of the following:

(a) marked impairment in the use of multiple non-verbal behaviors such as eye-to-eye gaze, facial expression, body postures, and gestures to regulate social interaction

(b) failure to develop peer relationships appropriate to developmental level

(c) a lack of spontaneous seeking to share enjoyment, interests, or achievements with other people (e.g., by a lack of showing, bringing, or pointing out objects of interest)

(d) lack of social or emotional reciprocity

(2) qualitative impairments in communication as manifested by at least one of the following:

(a) delay in, or total lack of, the development of spoken language (not accompanied by an attempt to compensate through alternative modes of communication such as gesture or mime)

(b) in individuals with adequate speech, marked impairment in the ability to initiate or sustain a conversation with others

(c) stereotyped and repetitive use of language or idiosyncratic language

(d) lack of varied, spontaneous make-believe play or social imitative play appropriate to developmental level

(3) restricted repetitive and stereotyped patterns of behavior, interests, and activities, as manifested by at least one of the following:

(a) encompassing preoccupation with one or more stereotyped and restricted patterns of interest that is abnormal either in intensity or focus

(b) apparently inflexible adherence to specific, nonfunctional routines or rituals

(c) stereotyped and repetitive motor mannerisms (e.g., hand or finger flapping or twisting, or complex whole-body movements)

(d) persistent preoccupation with parts of objects

B. Delays or abnormal functioning in at least one of the following areas, with onset prior to age 3 years: (1) social interaction, (2) language as used in social communication, or (3) symbolic or imaginative play.

C. The disturbance is not better accounted for by Rett's Disorder or Childhood Disintegrative Disorder. [Reprinted with permission from the American Psychiatric Association.]

The DSMIV also presents a description of **299.80**

Pervasive Developmental Disorder Not Otherwise Specified (Including Atypical Autism):

This category should be used when there is a severe and pervasive impairment in the development of reciprocal social interaction or verbal and nonverbal communication skills, or when stereotyped behavior, interests, and activities are present, but the criteria are not met for a specific Pervasive Developmental Disorder, Schizophrenia, Schizotypal Personality Disorder, or Avoidant Personality Disorder. For example, this category includes "atypical autism"—presentations that do not meet the criteria for Autistic Disorder because of late age at onset, atypical symptomatology, or subthreshold symptomatology, or all of these. [Reprinted with permission from the American Psychiatric Association.]

Other disorders having characteristics in common with autism:

• **Asperger Syndrome**…Symptoms include coordination deficits, depression, repetitive speech, monotonic voice, dislike of change, like of routine and rituals, inability to relate "normally" to people. Most individuals have IQ scores in the normal range.

• **Fragile-X Syndrome**…A genetic condition in which there is a constriction on the long arm of the X chromosome. Most individuals with Fragile-X Syndrome have mild to moderate retardation. Often present are repetitive motor behaviors, oversensitivity to sound, dysfunction in verbal and nonverbal communication, and cognitive processing problems.

• **Landau-Kleffner Syndrome**…Children develop normally for the first three to seven years, and then there is a rapid loss of language skills. Often these children are misdiagnosed as deaf. EEG readings are used to determine whether or not a person has Landau-Kleffner Syndrome. Autistic-like behaviors include attention deficits, insensitivity to pain, echolalic speech, and impaired motor skills.

• **Moebius Syndrome**…Causes many nervous system problems (including paralysis of the facial muscles, which leads to vision and speech difficulties) as well as behavioral problems like those associated with autism.

• **Rett Syndrome**…Usually seen in girls. Symptoms include loss of speech, loss of voluntary use of hands, hand-wringing movements, eating problems.

• **Sotos Syndrome**…Causes accelerated growth, enlargement of the skull, facial abnormalities, and often mental retardation. Autistic symptoms may include echolalia, head banging, twirling and spinning, as well as impaired social interaction skills.

• **Tourette Syndrome**…Characterized by involuntary tics such as eye blinking, shrugging, lip smacking, grunting, and cursing. Often present are anxiety attacks and a short attention span.

• **Williams Syndrome**…A rare disorder. Features are often described as "elf-like." Symptoms common to autism include developmental delays in language and gross motor skills, hypersensitivity to sounds, obsession, perseveration with objects, and rocking.

RESOURCES

American Association of University Affiliated Programs for Persons with Developmental Disabilities (AAUAP)
8630 Fenton St, Suite 410
Silver Spring, MD 20910
(301) 588-8252
A network of university-based and affiliated centers that diagnose and treat individuals with developmental disabilities such as autism.

Autism Research Foundation
Medical 10, Boston City Hospital
818 Harrison Av
Boston, MA 02118
Involved in the research of brain abnormalities in deceased individuals with autism. Sells a videotape about this research, titled "Autism…Challenges and Hope," (members of the Autism Society of America, $16; other $25). The Autism Research Foundation is not an information center for parents.

Autism Research Institute (ARI)
4182 Adams Av
San Diego, CA 92116
(619) 281-7165
Provides questionnaires used in research on diagnoses of autism in children (Forms E2 and E3). Single copies free. Publishes *Autism Research Review International*, a newsletter reporting the latest research on diagnosis and other aspects of autism.

Autism Society of America (ASA)
7910 Woodmont Av, Suite 650
Bethesda, MD 20814

(301) 657-0881/(800) 3AUTISM

Provides information on the diagnosis of autism. Publishes *The Advocate*, a quarterly newsletter on autism. Coordinates a network of affiliated local chapters.

CANDLE

4414 McCampbell Dr
Montgomery, AL 36106
Jane Rudick, Director. Disseminates information about Landau-Kleffner Syndrome and its treatment. Offers information packet for $5.00.

Cure Autism Now (CAN)

5225 Wilshire Blvd, Suite 226
Los Angeles, CA 90036
(213) 549-0500/(213) 549-0547 FAX

Portia Iversen, Director. An organization founded by parents who are dedicated to finding effective biological treatments and a cure for autism. CAN's mission is to fund medical research with direct clinical applications in the field of autism. CAN's Scientific Work Group is made up of top researchers and clinicians, many of whom are parents of children with autism. CAN believes that it is the parents who will mobilize the scientific and medical communities into action.

National Alliance for Autism Research (NAAR)

414 Wall St
Research Park
Princeton, NJ 08540
(888) 777-NAAR

Karen London, President. Founded by parents of children with autism, NAAR's mission is to encourage, promote, support, and fund biomedical research into the causes, prevention, treatment, and cure of the autistic spectrum

SUGGESTED READING

Allen, J., S. Baron-Cohen, and C. Gillberg. "Can autism be detected at 18 months? The needle, the haystack, and the CHAT," *British Journal of Psychiatry*, vol. 161, 1992, pp. 839-43. [Reviewed in *Autism Research Review International*, vol. 7, no. 1, 1993, p.1.]

Baird, G., S. Baron-Cohen, M. Bohman, M. Coleman, U. Frith, C. Gillberg, P. Howlin, G. Mesibov, T. Peters, E. Ritvo, S. Steffenburg, D. Taylor, L. Waterhouse, L. Wing, and M. Zapella, "Autism is not necessarily a pervasive developmental disorder" (letter), *Developmental Medicine*, vol. 33, no. 4, April, 1991, pp. 363-64. [Reviewed in *Autism Research Review International*, vol. 5, no. 2, 1991, p. 2.]

Baron-Cohen, Simon. *Mind Blindness: An Essay on Autism and Theory of Mind.* Cambridge, MA: MIT Press, 1995.

Blake, Allison. "Asperger's Syndrome: Is it autism?" *Autism Research Review International*, vol. 2, no. 4, 1988, pp. 1, 7.

du Verglas, Gabrielle. "Autism subgroups," *The Advocate*, vol. 19, no. 1, 1988, pp. 8-11, 19.

Frith, Uta [ed.]. *Autism and Asperger Syndrome.* Cambridge; NY: Cambridge University Press, 1991.

————. *Autism, Explaining the Enigma.* Cambridge, MA: Basil Blackwell, 1989.

Gillberg, Christopher [ed.]. *Diagnosis and Treatment of Autism.* New York and London: Plenum Press, 1989.

Gillberg, Christopher, and Mary Coleman. *The Biology of the Autistic Syndromes*, 2nd edition. Cambridge: Cambridge University Press.

Peschel, E., R. Peschel, C. W. Howe, J.W. [eds.]. *Neurobiological Disorders in Children and Adolescents.* San Francisco: Jossey-Bass. M.H.S. #54. (350 Sansome St., San Francisco, CA 94104, 415-433-1767.

Powers, Michael D. [ed.]. *Children With Autism: A Parent's Guide.* Rockville, MD: Woodbine House, 1989.

Rimland, Bernard. *Infantile Autism: The Syndrome and Its Implications for a Neural Theory of Behavior.* New York: Appleton Crofts, 1964. (Available through the Autism Research Institute.)

Schopler, Eric, and Gary Mesibov. *Diagnosis and Assessment in Autism.* New York: Plenum Press, 1988.

Tests

There are still no established guidelines defining what medical tests are important for the child diagnosed with autism. Often, children who have been diagnosed with autism are not given extensive laboratory work-ups. However, individuals with autism sometimes have underlying medical problems. Also, other disorders have been known to occur along with autism (Fragile-X Syndrome, Moebius Syndrome, William's Syndrome, to name a few). Dr. Christopher Gillberg, a child psychiatrist and pediatrician from Sweden, speaking at the 1990 Autism Society of America conference in Los Angeles, mentioned the many neurobiological factors that are associated with autism. These include, but are not limited to, epilepsy, tuberous sclerosis, neurofibromatosis, and mental retardation. He suggested the following procedures as part of a diagnostic work-up for autism:

1. A complete, detailed family history, looking for genetic abnormalities among family members. **History of the pregnancy, and child's medical history.**

2. Comprehensive, age-appropriate physical, medical, and neurodevelopmental examinations of the child.

3. Laboratory tests:

• **Chromosomal analysis**…with special regard to Fragile-X syndrome.

• **CAT-scan/or MRI scan**…looking for tuberous sclerosis, neurofibromatosis, hypomelanosis of Ito.

• **CSF-protein scan (cerebral spinal fluid)**…for amino-acids, particularly phenylaline, and CSF monoamines and endorphins.

• **EEG**…for epilepsy, brain damage.

• **Auditory brain stem response**…some children with such a dysfunction cannot tolerate music.

• **Hearing test**.

• **Complete vision exam**…at an early age, for if glasses are required, they would be more easily tolerated.

• **24-hour urinalysis**…including a metabolic screen, that checks for levels of uric acid and calcium.

• **Blood work-up**…for phenylalinine, uric acid, lactic acid, pyruvic acid, and a herpes titer.

Below is a list of tests which might indicate biochemical imbalances. It is reprinted with permission from Dr. Patricia Kane's book, *Food Makes the Difference*. It was not designed specifically for persons with autism, but it may be a useful guide for those interested in medical testing for bio-chemical problems.

Biochemical Tests

Amino acid assay…to search for metabolic errors in amino acid patterns that are disturbing the mental and physical health of the patient.

Membrane lipid analysis and essential fatty acid profile…to search for errors in fatty acid metabolism that also may be disturbing the mental and physical health of the patient.

Blood Analysis…whole-blood vitamin panel (protazol or erythrocyte) broad-spectrum chemistry screen.

Immune competency testing…immune testing for T and B cells, immunoglobulins, complements, immune complexes, null cells, PGF2A, and T helper/suppressor ratios, which offer information regarding the strengths and weaknesses of the patient's immune system.

Glucose-tolerance test and insulin levels…blood-sugar/insulin evaluation.

Hair analysis…to screen for the presence of heavy (toxic) metals and mineral imbalances.

Heidelberg gastrogram…to check for endocrine dysfunction.

Cytoscan…intracellular mineral evaluation to measure mineral deficiencies or imbalances on the cellular level.

Lactose-tolerance test… to test for an individual's ability to handle milk sugar (lactose).

Infectious assessment…to determine if *Candida albicans* or other fungi or bacteria are interfering with the health of the individual through infection.

Enzyme studies…erythrocyte transketolase, erythrocyte glutathione reductase, and so on for coenzyme activities.

Urinalysis… for evidence of the mauve factor indicating pyroluria, glucose, ketones, and other abnormalities.

There is an increasing awareness of the importance of **vision exams** for children with disabilities. Vision is more than being able to see things clearly. It involves eye coordination, perception and processing, focusing, tracking, and more. It is important for a child to be examined by a developmental optometrist who can check for developmental problems related to vision, not just acuity. Dr. Frederic Flach's book, *Rickie*, (briefly) discusses the breakthrough his daughter, who had been diagnosed with schizophrenia, experienced after vision problems were correctly diagnosed by Dr. Melvin Kaplan. Many parents of autistic children have reported good success with vision training, which is practiced by only a small proportion of developmental or behavioral optometrists.

RESOURCES

The Center for Visual Management
Dr. Melvin Kaplan, OD
150 White Plains Rd
Tarrytown, NY 10591
(914) 631-1070
Dr. Kaplan specializes in developmental vision problems, and is one of the leading authorities in this field.

Optometric Extension Program Foundation
1921 E. Carnegie Av, Suite 3-L
Santa Ana, CA 92705-5510
(949) 250-8070/(949) 250-8157 FAX
A nonprofit foundation for education and research in vision.

Can provide a free catalog as well as a referral list of developmental optometrists.

Parents Active for Vision Education (PAVE)
9620 Chesapeake Dr, Suite 105
San Diego, CA 92123
(619) 467-9620/(619) 467-9624 (FAX)
A nonprofit resource and support organization whose mission is to raise public awareness of learning related vision problems and the crucial relationship between vision and achievement. Can send a free pamphlet. Sells a video, "Vision Alert: 20/20 is not Enough!" for $35.

Irlen Institute
5380 Village Rd
Long Beach, CA 90808
(562) 496-2550/(562) 429-8699 FAX
Helen Irlen, Director. The Irlen Treatment Method is a "Perceptual Therapy" and is not a form of optometry or vision training. The Irlen Method utilizes colored filters worn as glasses to reduce or eliminate perception difficulties and sensory overload. Works extensively with individuals with autism. Affiliated clinics worldwide.

SUGGESTED READING

Task Force on the Future of Visual Developmental/Performance. "The efficacy of optometric vision therapy," *Journal of the American Optometric Association*, vol. 59, no. 2, 1988, pp. 95-105.

Caramagno, Liz. "A Diagnostic work-up for autism," *The Advocate*, vol. 24, no. 1, 1992, pp. 13, 14. (Summary of Dr. Gillberg's 1990 presentation to the Autism Society of America.)

Flach, Frederic. *Rickie.* New York: Fawcett Columbine, 1990.

Gillberg, Christopher, and Mary Coleman. *The Biology of the Autistic Syndrome.* Cambridge: Cambridge University Press, 1992.

Irlen, Helen. *Reading by the Colors.* Garden City Park, NY: Avery Publishing, 1991.

Kane, Patricia. *Food Makes the Difference.* New York: Simon and Schuster, 1985.

Kaplan, M., S. Edelson, J. Lydia Seip. "Behavioral changes in autistic individuals as a result of wearing ambient transitional prism lenses," *Child Psychiatry and Human Development*, vol. 29, Fall 1998, pp. 65-76.

Kaplan, Melvin. "Visual model for children with neurointegrative dysfunction," *The Advocate,* vol. 27, no. 1, 1995, pp. 25-26.

Rose, Marcy, and Nancy G. Torgerson, "A behavioral approach to vision and autism," *Journal of Optometric Vision Development,* vol. 25, no. 4, 1994, pp. 269-75.

Schulman, Randy L., "Optometry's role in the treatment of autism," *Journal of Optometric Vision Development,* vol. 25, no. 4, 1994, pp. 259-68.

Education

As with all children, educating the person with autism is a challenge! Part of this challenge stems from the fact that autism presents itself in so many different ways. Some children have remarkable skills, some are labeled retarded, some express themselves in aggressive ways, some are content to rock away in a world of their own. The population of individuals with autism holds to no set pattern of behavior. Each child presents his or her own unique behaviors and personality. Yet children with autism can be educated and have the legal right to be. Children with autism need a program that can provide individually appropriate instruction, social interaction, and development, as well as support and respect.

Federal Law in the United States

In the past, parents were given few options regarding the education of their child with disabilities. Often, parents were advised to put their child in an institution and "move on" with their lives. Some parents were able to afford private schools, in which their child had a better chance of receiving some stimulation and personal help. Others were not so fortunate. Today, options have greatly expanded. Now, in the United States, children with disabilities are guaranteed a free public education, thanks to pioneering parents and advocates who pushed the passage of The Education for All Handicapped Act (EHA) of 1975 (better known as Public Law 94-142). This law was updated in 1990, and it is now known as The Individuals With Disabilities Education Act (IDEA, Public Law 101-476).

Under the updated federal law, autism is categorized as a disability in its own right, and individuals with autism are now, specifically, entitled to receive an appropriate education. Under the law, states that provide a special education program meeting federal standards are granted funding from the federal government. The IDEA does not guarantee that a child will be educated in an ideal environment. The law only sets minimum requirements that states must comply with in order to receive funding. Consequently, the quality of special education services varies greatly from state to state.

The law mandates that children with disabilities are entitled to **special education and related services**. Special education means that the instruction afforded the child must be designed to meet the unique needs of each child. Instruction might take place in a classroom, home setting, private school, hospital, or institution. In other words, the child is entitled to receive an education in the environment that is most appropriate for him or her. Children also have the right to be educated in the **least restrictive environment**. That is, they are entitled to be educated with children who are not handicapped. It is up to the parents and school staff to determine how much inclusion or "mainstreaming" is possible for each individual child. Inclusion refers to the amount of time a child with a disability is educated with children without disabilities.

Currently, there is much debate among parents and educators about the topic of inclusion. There is a growing movement that we, as a society, should be moving toward full inclusion. Proponents of full inclusion feel services and education should integrate everyone regardless of the handicapping condition. However, there are just as many parents and educators who feel that this idea, though noble, would simply not be realistic or appropriate for some children. Again, parents, school staff, and others must work together to determine the programs and placements that best fit the unique needs of the child.

Related services are services provided by the school district that are needed for the child to benefit from the special education program. These services may include, but are not limited to, transportation, speech therapy, audiology, occupational or physical therapy, vision services, vocational services, individual instructional assistants, special equipment, and more.

Under the law, each child must have an **Individualized Education Program (IEP)**. The IEP is a written plan which must be in effect 30 days after a child has been evaluated and determined eligible for special education services. This plan is a blueprint for the educational services the child is to receive during the school year. It is developed according to the unique needs of the child, and it is updated at least yearly. The IEP is developed by a team and must include parental involvement as well as representation from the school district (teachers, administrators, school psychologist, speech therapist, etc.). Parents may call an IEP meeting at any time if they are not satisfied with their child's program or progress or if they wish to make changes in the goals and objectives of the plan. According to the Oregon Advocacy Center, the IEP must include:

- present level of performance (a statement of what the child can do);

[Author's note: This includes different areas, such as gross and fine motor skills, communication skills, cognitive skills, etc.]

- a statement of annual goals and short-term objectives;

- a statement of the special education and related services to be provided, including the amount of time and description of each related service;

- a statement of the extent the child will participate in regular educational programs (with children without disabilities) and any modifications of those programs needed to permit the child to participate;

- the date special education and related services will begin and how long these services are expected to continue;

- criteria, evaluation procedures and schedules for determining (at least once a year) whether the short-term objectives are met;

- a statement of needed services for transition to community living and employment for all students 16 and older, and for younger students when appropriate. [Broadhurst et al., 1991, p. 8.]

Parents and their children with disabilities now have many rights, but they must become aware of what those rights are and how to exercise them. Parents should become aware of what services their school districts provide. Parents often need to challenge their school districts to improve the quality of services provided. Parents can attend workshops on the legal aspects of special education, get in touch with advocacy groups, join a local chapter of the Autism Society of America, and ask anybody and everybody questions. Read the law, and learn how to quote it when necessary. Slowly but surely, one can gain confidence advocating for a child with a disability.

Early Intervention/Teaching Strategies

One thing most professionals do agree upon is how critical early intervention is for children with autism and other disabilities. It appears that intensive intervention at an early age increases the chances of "normal functioning" for some children with autism. In 1986, The Education of the Handicapped Amendments (Public Law 99-457) mandated early intervention services. Many states have begun early intervention services for children from birth to age three. Under the law, children ages three to five must be provided with the same services the school district provides for older children who qualify for special education services.

An **Individual Family Services Plan (IFSP)** is similar to an Individual Education Plan (IEP) but is designed for the child who qualifies for early intervention services. The IFSP is generally broader in scope than an IEP, including services for the family, such as home consultations, family training, case management services, speech or physical therapy, and classroom options. Early intervention may include help with language skills, social skills, cognitive skills, and/or behavior problems. The purpose of these programs is to reduce the effects of handicaps that may hinder development in small children. Early intervention can occur in any number of settings: at home, in schools, or in centers specializing in the treatment of autism, or in a combination of settings.

O. Ivar Lovaas and his team at the University of California at Los Angeles published a report documenting their successful treatment of autism with a highly structured behavior modification program for three-year olds. After two years of treatment, 42% of the subjects in an experimental group made major gains in intellectual and social development, and 47% of the children were mainstreamed successfully and were considered to be "indistinguishable from average children on tests of intelligence and adaptive behavior." [See McEachin et al.] Also, the book *Let Me Hear Your Voice*, by Catherine Maurice, is a well-documented account of one family's experience with the Lovaas method and of how this treatment successfully helped two of their children recover from autism.

Other centers, such as the TEACCH program in North Carolina, also provide intensive intervention programs by trained staff and parents. The TEACCH program seeks to improve an individual's skills in a structured educational environment. Home or school environments are sometimes modified to better accommodate the needs of the individual with autism. For instance, visual aids or cues are one such modification that may help those with autism better understand schedules, transitions, and expectations. Many schools have incorporated strategies designed by the TEACCH program into classrooms where children with autism are taught, and parents often carry similar strategies into the home setting. The TEACCH program provides in-service training for parents and teachers worldwide.

While one-on-one teaching strategies have been employed with success, there are also programs in which group teaching has been beneficial. One such method, called "Daily Life Therapy," pioneered by Dr. Kiyo Kitahara at the Higashi School in Japan, provides an education based on integration with nonhandicapped children and emphasizes rigorous physical education and the arts. [See Roland et al.]

Educational programs must be chosen with care. Parents will need to gather as much information as they can when choosing the best option for their child. Parents can check with their school district's special education department for a list of programs that may be appropriate for their child. The book *Children With Autism*, edited by Michael Powers, is an excellent resource guide for parents. (See suggested reading.) Also, some of the organizations listed at the end of this chapter offer excellent informational services.

Many books have been written about possible techniques for teaching children with autism, who can be especially difficult to educate. They may exhibit distracting behaviors, which interfere with learning, and they may lack the motivation to learn typically seen in other children. Behavior management techniques, designed to work with such difficulties, have a strong record of success in the education of people with autism.

Behavior management, or applied behavior analysis, refers to a method of teaching individuals with disabilities, including those with autism. Applied behavior analysis can be an effective teaching technique in many ways. It is not only a strategy that focuses on changing undesirable behaviors; it is also a technique for teaching tasks or skills. For instance, a desired skill might be analyzed and divided into smaller parts. These parts might be taught to an individual slowly, using reinforcers until the skill is learned. Parts of skills may be learned separately and then chained together. Behavioral programs should strive to integrate strategies for teaching new skills and managing behaviors considered problematic because skills and behaviors interact and influence each other.

First, behaviors are observed and analyzed. Then strategies for changing the behavior are attempted and results are monitored to see if the approach is effective. Some programs focus primarily on positive reinforcements ("nonaversives," such as praise or rewards) when the desired behavior is observed. Other programs incorporate punishment ("aversives") as well as positive reinforcers to minimize problem behaviors.

Whether or not to include punishment in a child's program is part of an ongoing debate among educators. There has been tremendous change in this field even in the last ten years. New terms such as "nonaversive behavior management" and "positive behavior support" are emerging in the literature. [See Horner et al.] Since all individuals with autism are unique and need specific teaching, programs for teaching each one should be unique. Parents should understand the philosophy of a program they are considering for their child and feel comfortable with it.

The New Jersey Center for Outreach and Services for the Autism Community, Inc. (COSAC) has developed an excellent set of guidelines for programs designed to educate individuals with autism. They are reprinted here, with permission, from COSAC's handbook, "Autism: Basic Information":

A SUMMARY OF PROGRAMMATIC REQUIREMENTS FOR INDIVIDUALS WITH AUTISM

• **Early diagnosis and appropriate intervention** are vital to the development of individuals with autism.

• **Highly structured, skill-oriented teaching and treatment programs** (programs which simultaneously address skill deficits and problem behaviors by utilizing both skill building and behavior reduction techniques throughout the day), based upon the principles of applied behavior analysis, are the most effective in improving the skills and behavior of individuals with autism.

• **Programs must be tailored to the specific needs of the individual** and delivered in a comprehensive, consistent, systematic, and coordinated manner. Since many children and adults with autism have deficits in many skill areas, providing comprehensive instruction is necessary.

• **Programs should be data-based.** Behaviors should be operationally defined. Teaching and treatment procedures should be outlined. The occurrence of behavior should be recorded before (baseline), during, and after (follow-up) the implementation of teaching and treatment procedures. A summary (i.e., graphs, charts) of data should be provided. Data-based programs permit objective evaluation of the effects of the intervention. On the basis of these data, programs should be revised as needed to assure continued progress.

• **Programs should use individualized motivational systems** (i.e., primary systems [food], token systems, behavior contracts, etc.) and appropriate reinforcement schedules (i.e., continuous, fixed ration, etc.). Motivational systems are based upon the learning principle that individuals tend to repeat or increase behaviors which are followed by positive consequences.

• **Teaching areas should be structured, organized, and distraction-free environments which incorporate intensive one-to-one and small group sessions. Schedules of routines and activities should proceed smoothly and reliably with and across days. Time spent "waiting" should be kept to a minimum.** Classrooms should be equipped with one-way mirrors for observation. For those individuals ready for transition to other settings, larger group sessions ("normal") classrooms should be provided.

• **To provide the consistency necessary for generalization** and maintenance of skills and appropriate behavior.

• Programs should be offered on a **full-day, year-round basis** from preschool through adulthood.

• **Individuals should be taught in multiple settings**, by multiple therapists using a variety of stimuli.

• **A comprehensive home programming/parent training program** should be provided to foster coordination of day and evening programming. Parents should be provided with support groups and extensive in-home behavior management training, which also gives parents a method of coping with many of the child's behavior problems.

• All personnel involved with individuals with autism should be extensively, specifically **trained and continuously evaluated**. On-going skill-based staff training and evaluation are necessary to help ensure staff excellence.

Education is a life-long process. For children with autism, education is critical and should begin as early as possible in a highly-structured, well-designed program. Parents must choose carefully the type of program that will best suit the needs of their child. Finally, parents and teachers must work together to provide a positive, supportive, and consistent learning environment for the individual with autism.

RESOURCES

Autism Research Institute
4182 Adams Av
San Diego, CA 92116
(619) 281-7165
Bernard Rimland, Director. Maintains referral lists of schools and other facilities for children and adults with autism. Provides information and publications on a wide variety of subjects concerning autism. Publishes the *Autism Research Review International*, a quarterly newsletter reporting on the latest research in the field of autism.

Autism Society of America (ASA)
7910 Woodmont Av, Suite 650
Bethesda, MD 20814
(301) 657-0881/(800) 3AUTISM

Contact for information about support groups in your locale. The ASA Information and Referral Service is a clearinghouse for information about autism, and services for those with autism. Publishes quarterly newsletter, *The Advocate*.

Burger School for the Autistic

30922 Beechwood
Garden City, MI 48135
(734) 762-8420
The largest school program in the nation specializing in the education of children with autism, operating since 1973. Has developed guides for teachers covering curriculum, behavior management, classroom structures, and more. Free brochure.

Eden Institute

One Logan Dr
Princeton, NJ 08540
(609) 987-0099
The Eden Family of Services includes a 12-month family-oriented school, group homes, employment opportunities, consultation and evaluation services as well as professional training workshops.

Indiana Resource Center for Autism (IRCA)

Institute for the Study of Developmental Disabilities
Indiana University
2853 E 10th St
Bloomington, IN 47408-2601
(812) 855-6508
Offers many excellent materials in print and video. Continually revises and updates resource materials for teachers, parents, and service providers. Write for a complete list of titles and costs.

Judevine Center for Autism
9455 Rott Rd.
St. Louis, MO 63127
(314) 849-4440
Offers a three-week training program for parents and professionals wanting to learn the Judevine Method for working with children with autism. Can send an information packet on request.

Division TEACCH
The University of North Carolina
310 Medical School Wing E
Chapel Hill, NC 27599-7180
(919) 966-2174
Dr. Gary Mesibov, Director. TEACCH stands for Treatment and Education of Autistic and Related Communications Handicapped Children. Offers parent and teacher training workshops and outreach services. Call for information.

Language and Cognitive Development Center (LCDC)
PO Box 270/11 Wyman St
Boston, MA 02130
(617) 522-5434
Arnold Miller and Eileen Eller-Miller, Founders. A nonprofit, accredited school and clinic for the education and treatment of children with autism and PDD. Their Oversight Program provides a range of services to public schools and parents distant from the Center.

New Breakthroughs
PO Box 25228
Eugene, OR 97402-0447
(541) 741-5070/(541) 896-0123 FAX
Carol Lee Berger, Owner. Offers several books on facilitated communication, instructional videos, as well as reading and

writing programs. Carol Lee Berger also give workshops and lectures nationwide. Write or call for information.

Project PACE
9725 SW Beaverton Hillsdale Hwy, Suite 230
Beaverton, OR 97005
(503) 643-7015
Dr. Katherine A. Calouri, Director. PACE stands for Personalizing Autistic Children's Education. Provides individualized instruction based on the principles of behavior modification, or applied behavioral analysis. Offers direct intervention, consultations, and workshops nationwide.

Research and Training Center on Positive Behavioral Support
The University of Oregon
RTC Secretary
Specialized Training Program
Eugene, OR 97403-1235
This center is a five-year project organized through the University of Oregon with five other major universities. Can send a detailed list of research reports, review papers, curriculum materials, and books.

Scientific Learning Corporation
1995 University Av, Suite 400
Berkeley, CA 94704
(888) 665-9707/(510) 665-9700
www. scientificlearning.com
Dr. Michail Merzenich and Dr. Paula Tallal, Founders. Scientific Learning's approach teaches language learning impaired children to process speech more efficiently, building skills they need to comprehend and use language more effectively. FastForword, CD-ROM and Internet-based training programs.

University of California at Los Angeles
Dr. O. Ivar Lovaas
Department of Psychology,1285 Franz Hall
UCLA
405 Hilgard Av
Los Angeles, CA 90024-1563
(310) 825-2319/ (310) 206-6173 FAX
Behavioral treatment programs for children with autism. Provides outreach services, parent training programs, and private training at UCLA. Provides an information packet regarding programs on request.

University of Kansas
Dr. Ann Turnbull
Beach Center on Families and Disability
3136 Haworth Hall
University of Kansas
Lawrence, KS 66045
(913) 864-7600
Provides publications catalog regarding behavioral support issues specifically geared toward families. Works in conjunction with the University of Oregon.

SUGGESTED READING
Books

Anderson, Winifred., and Stephen R. Chitwood. *Negotiating the Special Education Maze*. Rockville, MD: Woodbine House, 1990.

Bellack, Allan S., Michael Hersen, and Alan E. Kazdin [eds.]. *International Handbook of Behavior Modification and Therapy*. New York: Plenum Publishing, 1990.

Berkell, Diane [ed.]. *Autism: Identification , Education, and*

Treatment. 365 Broadway, Hillsdale, NJ 07642: Erlbaum Publishers, 1992.

Broadhurst, Mary E., and Suzy Harris. *Special Education: A Guide for Parents and Advocates*. Portland, OR: Oregon Advocacy Center, 1991. (Pamphlet.)

Cohen, Donald J., and Anne M. Donnellan. *Handbook of Autism and Pervasive Developmental Disorders*. New York: John Wiley and Sons, 1987.

Donnellan, Anne. *Classic Readings in Autism*. New York: College Park Press, 1985.

Gillingham, Gail. *Autism: Handle with Care.* Arlington, TX: Future Education, 1995.

Harris, Sandra L., and Jan S. Handleman [eds.]. *Aversive and Nonaversive Interventions*. New York: Springer Publishing, 1990.

Hodgdon, Linda. *Visual Strategies for Improving Communication.* Troy, MI: QuirkRoberts Publishing, 1997.

Holmes, David L. *Autism Through the Lifespan: The Eden Model.* Rockville, MD: Woodbine House, 1995.

Koegel, R.L., A. Rincover, and A.L. Egel. *Educating and Understanding Autistic Children*. San Diego: College-Hill, 1982.

Lovaas, O. Ivar. *Teaching Developmentally Disabled Children: The ME Book*. Austin, TX: Pro-Ed Publishers, 1980.

Maurice, Catherine. *Let Me Hear Your Voice*. New York: Alfred Knopf, 1993.

Powers, Michael. *Educating Children with Autism: A Guide to Selecting an Appropriate Program*. Rockville, MD: Woodbine House, 1995.

Schopler, Eric, Robert J. Reichler, and Margaret Lansing. *Individualized Assessment and Treatment for Autistic and*

Developmentally Disabled Children , vols.1 & 2. Baltimore: University Park Press, 1980.

Schreibman, Laura. *Autism*. 2111 West Hillcrest Dr, Newbury Park, CA 91320: Sage Publications, 1988.

Articles

Horner, Robert H., Glen Dunlap, Robert L. Koegel, Edward G. Carr, Wayne Sailor, Jacki Anderson, Richard W. Albin, and Robert E. O'Neill. "Toward a technology of 'nonaversive' behavioral support," *Journal of the Association for Persons with Severe Handicaps*, vol.15, no. 3, 1990, pp.125-32.

Koegel, Lynn K., Robert L. Koegel, Christine Hurley, and William D. Frea. "Improving social skills and disruptive behavior in children with autism through self-management," *Journal of Applied Behavior Analysis*, no. 2, Summer 1992, pp. 341-53.

McEachin, John J., and Ivar Lovaas. "Long-term outcome for children with autism who received early intensive behavioral treatment," *American Journal on Mental Retardation*, vol. 97, no. 4, Jan. 1993, pp. 359-91. [Reviewed in *Autism Research Review International,* vol. 7, no. 1, 1993, pp.1, 6.]

Roland, C.C., G.G. McGee, T.R. Risley, and B. Rimland. "Description of the Tokyo Higashi Program for autistic children," Autism Research Institute Publication #77, 1987.

Simpson, Richard L., and Gary M. Sasso, "Full inclusion of students with autism in general education settings: Values versus science," *Focus on Autistic Behavior*, vol. 7, no. 3, 1992, pp.1-13. [Reviewed in *Autism Research Review International*, vol. 6, no. 4, 1992, p.1.]

VitaminTherapy

B6/Magnesium Supplements

In the early 1960s, Dr. Bernard Rimland, now director of the Autism Research Institute, heard reports from parents of improvements seen in their children after taking certain vitamins. Dr. Rimland and other scientists investigated these claims and developed a vitamin and mineral therapy which is now considered an effective treatment for some individuals with autism. Researchers concluded that large doses of vitamin B6 (pyridoxine), in combination with magnesium and other vitamins and minerals, are an effective treatment for 45-50% of the individuals with autism who try it. Many scientific, double-blind studies verify the effectiveness of this treatment. [See Rimland, Form Letter.]

Vitamin B6 and magnesium are water soluble and therefore are not stored in body fat. It is important to take vitamin B6 in combination with other vitamins and minerals in order to help metabolize vitamin B6 and magnesium.

Currently, Kirkman Laboratory produces a relatively inexpensive mega-B6/magnesium supplement, in both caplet and powder form. The caplets are easier to manage than the powder, but if the individual cannot swallow caplets, the powder may be mixed with food or liquids. The supplement contains no artificial colors, preservatives, starch, or yeast. The Kirkman formula also provides many other essential vitamins and nutrients, making it superior to B6 and magnesium alone.

The goal of vitamin therapy is to normalize body metabolism and improve behavior. Studies have shown that vitamin B6 helps to normalize brain waves and urine chemistry, control hyperactivity, and improve overall behavior. It may also help in reducing the effects of allergic reactions by strengthening the immune system. Although improvements vary considerably among individuals, other possible improvements from B6/magnesium therapy are:

• speech improvements

• improved sleeping patterns

• lessened irritability

• increased span of attention

• greater desire for learning

• decrease in self-injury and self-stimulation

• overall improvement in general health. [See Rimland Form Letter.]

In some cases behavioral improvements can be seen in a matter of days. However, the vitamins often take 60-90 days to show any effects. Perseverance and consistency by both the parents and their children is required. Dosage is also an important consideration. The Autism Research

Institute provides a form letter on B6/magnesium therapy that includes a detailed description of the treatment, a dosage chart, a table of scientific research data, and an extensive bibliography. Reading this report before beginning the megavitamin therapy is recommended.

Dimethylglycine (DMG) Supplements

Despite its technical name, Dimethylglycine (DMG), is a food substance. Its chemical make-up resembles that of water soluble vitamins, specifically vitamin B15. DMG does not require a prescription, and it can be purchased at many health food stores. The most common form of DMG is a tiny (125 mg) tablet wrapped in foil. The tablet is pleasant tasting and dissolves rapidly in the mouth. A box of thirty tablets costs about $9.50.

Anecdotal reports from parents giving their child DMG indicate improvements in the areas of speech, eye contact, social behavior, and attention span. A small child may be given half a 125 mg tablet per day, with breakfast, for a few days. For a larger child, one tablet a day should be given until results are noted. The amount may be increased to one or two tablets a day for a child and two or three tablets per day for an adult. Occasionally, if too much DMG is given, the child's activity level has been noted to increase; otherwise, there are no apparent side effects. [See Rimland, "Dimethylglycine (DMG) in the Treatment of Autism."]

RESOURCES

Autism Research Institute
4182 Adams Av
San Diego, CA 92116
(619) 281-7165
Bernard Rimland, Director. Has published extensive information on the subject of vitamin supplements in the treatment of autism. Request their publications list. Form 39E deals specifically with B6/magnesium therapy.

HRI Pfeiffer Treatment Center
1804 Centre Pointe Dr, Suite 102
Naperville, IL 60563
(630) 505-0300
An outpatient medical facility specializing in biochemical testing, diagnosis, and individualized nutrient therapy for children and adults. Treatment is based on health history, physical exam, and extensive laboratory analysis. The treatment program consists of vitamins, minerals, and amino acids that are specifically selected and dosed to address the individual's chemical imbalances.

KareMor® International
PO Box 21858
Phoenix, AZ 85036-1858
(800) 582-5273
Offers a variety of Vitamist® spray nutrients. Call for brochure.

Kirkman Sales Co.
PO Box 1009
Wilsonville, OR 97070
(503) 694-1600/(800) 245-8282
Provides a vitamin/mineral supplement containing high doses of B6 and magnesium as well as other essential vitamins and minerals.

Wholesale Nutrition
Box 3345
Saratoga, CA 95070
(408) 867-6368/(800) 325-2664
This company sells Dimethylglycine (DMG).

SUGGESTED READING

Books

Leklem, J., and R. Reynolds (eds.). *Vitamin B6 Responsive Disorders in Humans*. New York: Alan Liss, 1988.

Rimland, B. *Infantile Autism: The Syndrome and Its Implications for a Neural Theory of Behavior*. New York: Appleton Century Crofts, 1964.

Schopler, E., and G. Mesibov (eds.). *Neurobiological Issues In Autism*. New York: Plenum Press, 1987.

Articles

Coleman, M., G. Steinberg, J. Tippett, H.N. Bhagavan, D.B. Coursin, M. Gross, C. Lewis, and L.A. DeVeau. "A preliminary study of the effect of pyridoxine administration in a subgroup of hyperkinetic children: A double-blind crossover comparison with methylphenidate," *Biological Psychiatry*, vol. 141, 1979, pp. 741-51.

Lelord, G., J.P. Muh, C. Barthelemy, J. Martineau, B. Garreau and, E. Callaway. "Effects of pyridoxine and magnesium on autistic symptoms...Initial observations," *Journal of Autism and Developmental Disorders* , vol. 11, 1981, pp. 219-30.

Martineau, J., C. Barthelemy, and G. Lelord. "Long-term effects of combined vitamin B6-magnesium administration in an autistic child," *Biological Psychiatry*, vol. 21, 1986, pp. 511-18.

Rimland, Bernard. "Dimethylglycine (DMG) in the Treatment of Autism," Autism Research Institute Publication 110, 1991. (20¢)

———. "Form Letter Regarding High Dosage Vitamin B6 and Magnesium Therapy for Autism and Related Disorders." Autism Research Institute Publication 39, revised 1991. (50 ¢)

Rimland, B., E. Callaway, and P. Dreyfus. "The effects of high doses of vitamin B6 on autistic children: A double-blind crossover study," *American Journal of Psychiatry*, vol. 135, 1978, pp. 472-75.

Medications For Treating Autistic Symptoms

No primary medication is used to treat autism. Medications are usually prescribed to decrease specific symptoms associated with autism. These symptoms may include self-injurious behavior, aggressive behavior, seizures, depression, anxiety, hyperactivity, or obsessive-compulsive behavior. Medications alone are not a solution to the problems associated with autism. Individuals with autism need well rounded intervention, including behavior management strategies, environmental modifications, and positive support services. Parents wishing to try medications for their children should be given the support and knowledge necessary to maintain a safe level of treatment. Parents need to be aware of potential risks and harmful side effects, and should carefully weigh them against possible benefits before treatment begins. Dosage should be carefully considered and monitored. There must be good communication between parents, physicians, service providers, and school personnel to monitor treatment with any medication. Accurate data on the effects of medication are also essential. [See Gray, pp. 1-4.]

Listed below are the various classifications of medications used to treat symptoms associated with autism.

• **Antipsychotics**…Also known as neuroleptics or "major" tranquilizers. Sometimes used to treat severe aggression, self-injurious behavior, agitation, or insomnia. Side effects may include tardive dyskinesia (an involuntary muscular twitching, which may become irreversible), also tremors, stiffness, and sleepiness. Medications include Mellaril™, Haldol™, Thorazine™, Risperdal™.

• **Anticonvulsants**…Given to control seizures. Side effects may include drowsiness, gum swelling, negative behavioral and cognitive performance. Medications include Tegretol™, Depakote™, Dilantin™.

• **Anti-anxiety**…Sometimes prescribed to relieve "nerves", anxiety, or anxiousness. Medications vary in effectiveness for long-term anxiety. Side effects associated with Valium™ and Librium™ may include increased behavior problems. Some antidepressants are used to treat chronic anxiety. They include Trofranil™ and Elavil™.

• **Antidepression, Antimania**…These medications are used to treat disorders such as depression, compulsive behaviors, mania, panic, or anxiety. Lithium™ and Depakote™ are sometimes prescribed for bipolar (manic-depressive) disorder. Anafranil™ and Prozac™ are sometimes prescribed for compulsive behavior. Most antidepressants take two to three weeks before effectiveness is noted. Side effects may include agitation, insomnia, decreased appetite, hyperactivity.

• **Beta Blockers**…These medications are usually used to control blood pressure, but are sometimes given to individuals to decrease aggression or hyperactivity caused by a rush of adrenaline. The beta blockers help to prevent the adrenalin rush and allow the individual to control impulsive reactions. Medications include Inderal™ and Clonidine/ Catapres™. May cause drowsiness, irritability, lowered blood pressure.

• **Opiate Blockers**…Some researchers theorize that self-injurious behaviors may cause the brain to release endorphins (chemicals which produce an opiate-like "high"), which may cause the individual to continue the self-injury in order to feel good. Opiate-blockers act to block the pleasurable sensation and allow the individual to feel the pain. As a result, self-injury may diminish. Sometimes, a sedating effect has been noted. Naltrexone/Trexan™ is an opiate blocker. These drugs may also improve socialization and general well-being.

• **Sedatives**…Given to individuals who have difficulty sleeping. Often medication is gradually withdrawn when normal sleep patterns are established. If the medication is not suitable for an individual it can cause excitation or sleeplessness. Chloral Hydrate™, Noctec™, and Benedryl™ are examples of sedatives.

• **Stimulants**…Sometimes prescribed for hyperactivity and attention or concentration problems. Side effects may include decreased appetite, sadness, tantrums, and hyperactivity after medication wears off. Ritalin™ and Dexedrine™ are stimulants.

Medications can sometimes help an individual with autism by providing relief from specific symptoms that interfere with daily life. Their use should be carefully monitored both by parents and professionals caring for the individual with autism. See table on page 50 regarding parental ratings of drug interventions.

RESOURCES

Autism Research Institute (ARI)

4182 Adams Av
San Diego, CA 92116
(619) 281-7165

Dr. Bernard Rimland, Director. Publishes *Autism Research Review International*, a newsletter which summarizes the latest research on medications used in the treatment of individuals with autism. Can provide a bibliography of reading materials and articles on this subject. Collects data from parents on the effectiveness of such medications used to treat autism. Offers for $25.00 the Defeat Autism Now! (DAN!) Clinical Options Manual. The DAN! manual is designed to refer physicians to the most appropriate medical tests (including preferred laboratories) and treatment options for individuals with autism and related disorders. The DAN! manual represents the consensus of a panel of carefully selected experts convened by the Autism Research Institute.

Secretin Therapy

Secretin is a digestive hormone which also plays a part in brain functioning, including stimulating and regulating the neurotransmitter serotonin. Secretin, as a prescription drug, must be administered by a physician. The safety and efficacy of treating autistic symptoms with secretin is not yet known. The Autism Research Institute offers a booklet, "Unlocking the Potential of Secretin." It is available for $15.00. Also, information can be accessed on the internet: www.secretin.com

IVIG Therapy/Dr. Sudhir Gupta

University of California
Medical Sciences I, Room C-240
Irvine, CA 92717
(714) 824-5818/FAX (714) 824-4362
Intravenous Immune Globulin (IVIG) is a therapy used to treat autoimmune disorders and immune deficiency syndromes. Patient must undergo immunologic screening to determine whether treatment is indicated.

SUGGESTED READING

Berkell, D.E. [ed.]. *Autism: Identification, Education, and Treatment*. Hillsdale, NJ: Lawrence Erlbaum Associates, 1992.

Gillberg, Christopher [ed.]. *Diagnosis and Treatment of Autism*. New York and London: Plenum Press, 1989.

Gray, Linda. "Medication issues in autism," *Indiana Resource Center for Autism Newsletter*, vol. 6, no. 2, 1993, pp.1-4.

Grandin, Temple. "New drug treatments for autistic adults and adolescents," *The Advocate*, vol. 23, no. 3, 1991.

McDougle, C.J., J.P. Holmes, D.C. Carlson, G.H. Pelton, D.J. Cohen and L.H. Price. "A double-blind, placebo-controlled study of risperidone in adults with autistic disorder and other pervasive developmental disorders." *Archives of General Psychiatry*, vol. 55, no. 7, 1998, pp. 633-641.

Plioplys, Audrius. "Intravenous immunoglobulin treatment of children with autism." *Journal of Child Neurology*, vol. 13, 1998, pp. 79-82.

BIOLOGICAL INTERVENTIONS IN AUTISM
PARENT RATING OF BEHAVIORAL EFFECTS OF DRUGS, VITAMINS AND DIET

TREATMENT	NO. OF CASES	% WORSE	% NO EFFECT	% BETTER	ARI Form 34C BETTER: WORSE
Nystatin (Ketoconazole)[A]	74	3	45	53	17.667:1 c
Beta Blocker (Propranolol Corgard)	65	14	55	31	2.214:1
Tegretol[B]	265	18	46	35	1.944:1
Fenfluramine (Pondimin)	225	18	50	32	1.778:1
Deanol (Deaner)	142	16	58	26	1.625:1
Naltrexone (Trexan)	29	21	45	34	1.619:1
Lithium	86	26	34	41	1.577:1
Depakene (Valproic Acid)[B]	124	21	48	31	1.476:1
Prozac	55	31	27	42	1.355:1
Mellaril	1098	26	41	33	1.269:1
Trofanil (Imipramine)	107	29	36	36	1.241:1
Zorontin	30	30	33	37	1.233:1
Benadryl	701	21	54	25	1.190:1
Haldol (Haloperidol)	449	36	24	40	1.111:1
Stelazine	266	28	44	29	1.036:1
Dilantin[B]	610	26	48	26	1.000:1
Hydroxyzine (Vistaril/Atarax)	138	23	57	20	0.870:1
Thorazine (Chlorpromazine)	619	36	39	25	0.694:1
Valium (Diazepam)	386	32	46	22	0.688:1
Phenobarbital (Luminal)[B]	487	43	37	21	0.488:1
Cylert (Pemoline)	137	50	26	24	0.480:1
Ritalin	880	48	29	23	0.479:1
Amphetamine (Dexedrine)	439	51	29	20	0.392:1
Mysoline[B]	67	58	30	12	0.207:1
Ascorbic Acid (Vitamin C)	133	2	46	52	26.000:1 c
Folic Acid	135	2	52	46	23.000:1 c
Vitamin B6 (and magnesium)	852	5	48	47	9.400:1 c
Dimethylglycine (DMG)	194	6	54	40	6.667:1 c
Removed Milk Products	902	1	55	43	43.000:1 c
Removed Wheat	488	1	60	39	39.000:1 c
Removed Sugar	906	2	50	48	24.000:1 c
Rotation Diet	131	3	56	40	13.333:1 c

A. Nystatin and Ketoconazole are anti-fungal drugs useful only if autism is yeast-related.
B. Figure shows behavioral effects; anti-convulsant effects on following graph.
C. Better/worse ratio marked "c" are unstable due the small number of cases rated "worse". A small change in "worse"% changes the ratio greatly. "Worse" refers to "behavior." Drugs, but not vitamins or diet, typically also cause physical problems if used long-term.

Dietary Interventions

The role diet and allergies play in the life of a child or adult with autism is probably one of the most significant, yet least understood areas of treatment. This means that parents who want to explore this avenue of treatment must really do their homework. Extensive reading is required. Finding a competent professional with whom you feel comfortable may take some time. It is the rare MD who has had any nutritional training whatsoever. This may mean finding a doctor who specializes in orthomolecular medicine, a naturopathic physician, or a doctor who has been trained in nutrition. Finally, commitment and perseverance are required to make dietary changes and stick with them. Luckily, there are now many excellent books available on diet, food sensitivities, and allergies.

In the book, *Fighting For Tony*, author and mother Mary Callahan let the world know about the possible connection of cerebral allergies and autism. Her son, diagnosed with autism, improved dramatically over time after cow's milk was eliminated from his diet. The term "cerebral allergy" refers to the effect a food intolerance may have on the brain. This intolerance may cause the tissues of the brain to swell and become inflamed, much as the nose becomes red and irritated if one is allergic to pollen...but in the brain, we cannot see this swelling occur. The symptoms, however, may include disturbances of learning and behavior.

Although any food could be an offender, there are several foods that are considered prime suspects in causing behavior disturbances. Sugar is one. Not only are some children allergic to it, they may suffer from an inability to metabolize it properly. In this condition, known as "relative hypoglycemia," blood sugar levels drop too fast after a person consumes foods containing simple sugars or simple carbohydrates. Hypoglycemia may also be triggered by an allergic reaction. As a result, the adrenal glands in the body become stressed and depleted, and over time cease to function normally. The effects of hypoglycemia may include mood swings, irrational behavior, irritability, sleep disturbances, nervousness, and the list goes on.

Other foods that cause allergic reactions are, unfortunately, foods we often consume the most. Wheat is one such food. Some children cannot tolerate even the smallest amount of wheat without their behavior becoming unmanageable. Milk, as in the case of Tony, has been linked over and over to behavior problems. Other common food offenders include corn, chocolate, chicken, tomatoes, and certain fruits. However, any food can cause an intolerance or sensitivity. The key is uncovering the problem foods, and often there may be more than one.

Besides food, other substances may cause reactions in children. Hyperactivity has been linked to an intolerance to food additives, such as phosphates and food colorings.

Molds, chemicals, perfumes, and other substances may cause allergic reactions. Hyperactivity may also be caused by a lack of essential fatty acids in the diet. In addition, behavior and learning problems have been linked to the toxicity of heavy metals such as lead and aluminum. A hair-mineral analysis test may be beneficial in revealing heavy metal toxicity or deficiency of essential minerals.

Some research studies have indicated that individuals with autism may have trouble metabolizing peptides into amino acids because of an enzyme defect. Two sources of protein, gluten (found in wheat, rye, oats, and other cereals) and casein (protein from milk), are particularly suspect. [See Reichelt et al., pp. 308-19.] Urine samples of autistic subjects have also indicated a higher than normal level of peptides. [See Shattock et al., pp. 320-34.] Some success has been noted when diets were modified to exclude casein and gluten. [See Reichelt et al.] Guidelines for implementing a gluten and casein free diet program can be ordered through the Autism Research Institute.

Where is the best place to begin? Start by eliminating "junk" foods. Read labels on packaged and processed foods. You may be amazed at how much sugar is added to everything! Start improving your family's diet by serving fresh foods and foods that haven't been refined to the point where virtually all of the nutrients are gone. Also start observing your child. Is there a food he or she craves? Ironically, it is the food most often craved that may be causing allergic reactions.

There are ways to uncover allergies. Some tests are more effective than others at discovering intolerances to foods and chemicals. Careful research and consultation with a professional who is skilled in this area are probably your best bets in determining which tests are most appropriate.

More importantly, food intolerances can often be determined by beginning a rotation or an elimination diet and observing any changes in behavior. This is carried out at home and doesn't cost anything except time and the money for the food. Many of the books listed below discuss exactly how to begin a rotation diet and what sort of changes to look for. If possible, get the help of a professional, one who is *supportive* and *knowledgeable* about how food sensitivities can affect the nervous system.

At first, changes in diet may seem traumatic to everyone in the family. However, if an allergy is uncovered, treatment can be very successful. Approach the diet/allergy connection slowly, read as much as you can, and observe eating patterns in your own family. Try not to become overwhelmed with all the possibilities. Even small changes can sometimes bring significant results.

RESOURCES

Allergy-Induced Autism Support and Self-Help Group
3 Palmera Av, Calcot,
Reading, Berks, RG3 7DZ
United Kingdom
Tel: 0734 419460
Brenda O'Reilly (organizer and parent contact). Offers dietary information concerning children who may suffer from allergy-induced autism. Currently involved in a research study with Birmingham University (UK) looking for possible enzyme deficiencies in children with autism.

Association for Comprehensive NeuroTherapy
1128 Royal Palm Beach Blvd, #283
Royal Palm Beach, FL 33411
(561) 798-0472
http://www.latitudes.org

Links a variety of remedies and practices with a spectrum of disorders that have things in common with autism. Publishes the newsletter, *Latitudes*.

American Academy of Environmental Medicine (AAEM)
#10 E Randolph St
New Hope, PA 18938
(215) 862-4544
Publishes AAEM Directory of members. Provides educational aids, tapes, and audio-visual presentations on environmental medicine.

American Association of Naturopathic Physicians (AANP)
601 Valley St, Suite 105
Seattle, WA 98109
(206) 298-0125
Can provide a list of associated naturopathic physicians or refer you to a registered naturopathic physician in your area.

American Foundation for Alternative Health Care Research and Development
25 Landfield Av
Monticello, NY 12701
Serves as an alternative health care information center. Compiles data and statistics.

Analytical Research Labs
2225 West Alice
Phoenix, AZ 85021
(602) 995-1581
Can provide a hair analysis to check for toxic metals and mineral imbalances.

Autism Network for Dietary Intervention (ANDI)
PO Box 17711
Rochester, NY 14617-0711

e-mail: autismNDI@aol.com
http://www.autismNDI.com

Lisa Lewis and Karen Seroussi, Directors. Offers a newsletter and product catalogue for those interested in dietary interventions for children with autism and related disorders. Newsletter is $20 per year. *Special Diets for Special Kids*, a book by Lisa Lewis, can be ordered for $28.90.

Autism, Intolerance, and Allergy (AIA) a program of:
The Feingold Association of the United States (FAUS)
127 E Main St, #106
Riverhead, NY 11901
(800) 321-FAUS (3287)
www.feingold.org
Jean Curtain, Director. A program of the Feingold Association. AIA is a group of parents and medical professionals dedicated to investigating the biochemical origins of the autistic condition. Provides information on dietary intervention for children and adults with autism.

The Body Bio Center (BBC)
South 12th Street
PO Box 829
Millville, NJ 08332
(609) 825-8338
Patricia Kane, Director. A nonprofit organization offering biochemical intervention data to professionals and parents of children with prematurity, traumatic brain injury, and autism. Information packet available.

Feingold Association of the United States (FAUS)
PO Box 6550
Alexandria, VA 22306
(703) 768-FAUS
Promotes understanding of the dietary link between artificial

colors, flavors, preservatives, etc. and hyperactivity, learning, and behavior disorders. National organization with local chapters. Members receive a handbook, food list, and medication lists. Publishes a monthly newsletter.

Immuno Laboratories
1620 W Oakland Park Blvd
Ft. Lauderdale, FL 33311
(888) 423-8837
Dr. John Rebello, Director. A state, federal, and Medicare-licensed laboratory, Immuno offers comprehensive diagnostic programs in the fields of allergy, immunology, and nutrition. Tests include IgG, IgE (food allergy blood tests) as well as Candida Albicans Assay.

International Health Foundation
PO Box 3494
Jackson, TN 38303-3494
(901) 660-7090
William G. Crook, MD, President; author of many books concerning children with allergies, yeast imbalances, and hyperactivity. Can provide information on health and learning problems related to food, yeast overgrowth, and chemical sensitivities.

Practical Allergy Research Foundation
PO Box 60
Buffalo, NY 14223
(716) 875-5578
Dr. Doris Rapp, President. Seeks to enhance public awareness of allergies, their symptoms, and remedies. Fosters research in allergies. Produces and distributes teaching aids. Library of books and audio and video tapes.

SUGGESTED READING

Callahan, Mary. *Fighting for Tony*. New York: Simon & Schuster, 1987.

Crook, William. *Solving the Puzzle of Your Hard-To- Raise Child*. New York: Random House, 1987. (Available from Pedicenter Press, PO Box 3116, Jackson, TN 38301.)

Crowell, Beth and Andy. *Dietary Intervention as a Therapy in the Treatment of Autism and Related Disorders.* 1992. (Available from Beth and Andy Crowell, 208 South St, PO Box 801, Housatonic, MA 01236. $14.95+S&H.)

Fredericks, Carl. *Psycho-Nutrition*. New York: Grosset and Dunlap, 1976.

Hersey, Jane. *Why Can't My Child Behave?* 1996. (Available from Pear Tree Press, PO Box 30146 Alexandria, VA 22310. $22.00 ppd.)

Kane, Patricia. *Food Makes the Difference*. New York: Simon and Schuster, 1985.

Lewis, Lisa. *Special Diets for Special Kids*. Arlington, TX: Future Horizons. 1998. (800) 489-0727.

Mandell, M., and L. Scanlon. *Dr. Mandell's 5-Day Allergy Relief System*. New York: Thomas Y. Crowell, 1979.

Philpott, William H. *Brain Allergies*. New Canaan, CT: Keats Publishing, 1980.

Rapp, Doris. *Is This Your Child?* New York: William Morrow, 1991.

Reichelt, Karl, Ann-Mari Knivsberg, Gunnar Lind, and Magne Nodland. "Probable etiology and possible treatment of childhood autism," *Brain Dysfunction*, no. 4, 1991, pp. 308-19. [Reviewed in *Autism Research Review International*, vol. 7, no. 1, 1993, pp. 4-7.]

Shattock, Paul., and Gillian Lowdon. "Proteins, peptides, and autism: Part 2," *Brain Dysfunction*, no. 4, 1991, pp. 323-34. [Reviewed in *Autism Research Review International*, vol. 7, no. 1, 1993, pp. 4, 7.]

Weintraub, Skye. *Minding Your Body: A Comprehensive Guide to Healthy Living.* Portland, OR: Complimentary Publishing, 1995. (To order: (541) 345-0747.)

Williams, Katherine, Paul Shattock, and Thomas Berney. "Proteins, peptides and autism: Part 1," *Brain Dysfunction*, no. 4, 1991, pp. 320-22. [Reviewed in *Autism Research Review International*, vol. 7, no. 1, 1993, pp. 4,7.]

Some of the books listed above are available through the Autism Research Institute.

NOTE:

The **Autism Research Institute** (4182 Adams Av, San Diego, CA 92116) has several easy to read publications which give an overview of how food may be involved in the symptoms of autism. All written by Dr. Bernard Rimland (some co-authored), they include:

•"Megavitamins, Hypoglycemia, and Food Intolerances as Related to Autism" (60¢)

•"Angela Is Coming Home: Case History of Ecologic Diagnosis and Treatment of an Autistic Child" (60¢)

•"Hair Mineral Analysis and Behavior: An Analysis of the Literature" (65¢)

•"Nutritional Approaches to the Reduction of Delinquency, Criminality, and Violence" ($1)

•"The Feingold Diet: An Assessment of the Reviews by Mattes, by Kavale and Forness and Others" (40¢)

•"Healthy Children vs. Junk Food" (20¢)

•"An Orthomolecular Study of Psychotic Children" (50¢)

•"Vitamin and Mineral Supplementation as a Treatment for Autistic and Mentally Retarded Persons" ($1).

•"Allergy and Behavior Information Package." Six papers on allergies and food intolerance as related to autism, hyperactivity, seizures and learning disabilities ($4).

Anti-yeast Therapy

The possible link between *Candida albicans* and autism, as well as other learning disabilities, is a topic of debate in the medical community. Some doctors call the "yeast syndrome" a fad, while other doctors claim to have helped many children by reducing an overabundance of yeast or related organisms in their systems.

Candida is a yeast-like fungus that is normally present in the body to some degree. Certain circumstances, however, may lead to an overgrowth of yeast that a normal, healthy immune system would otherwise suppress. Common symptoms of such an overgrowth are vaginal yeast infections and thrush (white patches sometimes present in the mouth of an infant). More severe symptoms of yeast overgrowth may include long-term immune system disturbances, depression, schizophrenia, and possibly autism.

Medical Complaints Associated with the Candida Complex

• Intestinal problems (constipation, diarrhea, flatulence)

• Distended stomach

• Excessive genital touching in infants and young children

• Cravings for carbohydrates, fruits and sweets. After ingestion of carbohydrates, hyperactivity for 15-20 minutes followed by hypoactivity

• Unpleasant odor of hair and feet, acetone smell from the mouth

• Skin rashes

• Fatigue, lethargy, depression, anxiety

• Insomnia

• Behavior problems

• May act "drunk"

• Hyperactivity [From Rimland/Mayo Letter.]

Candida overgrowth is often attributed to long-term antibiotic or hormonal treatments. It has been reported that some children whose autistic tendencies surfaced at 18-24 months had been continually treated with antibiotics to control chronic ear infections. Other possible causes of candida overgrowth: immunosuppressant drug therapy, exposure to herpes or chicken pox, exposure to toxins that might disrupt the immune system.

It may be hard to find a physician who is knowledgeable or accepting of the possible link between candida and severe learning and developmental disorders such as autism.

However, Dr. Bernard Rimland of the Autism Research Institute has suggested that perhaps 5-10 % of children with autism whose medical profiles indicate the possibility of yeast overgrowth may see some improvement if properly treated for candida.

Doctors can recommend a stool analysis that tests for possible yeast overgrowth. Unfortunately, stool cultures are not always reliable. Doctors familiar with the treatment of yeast overgrowth will sometimes suggest a therapeutic trial of an antifungal medication. In this case, treatment is based on medical history or current symptoms that may indicate a yeast overgrowth. The patient is carefully monitored to see if the medication is useful.

Treatment for candida overgrowth usually includes prescription of an antifungal medication. Nystatin is commonly prescribed, but others are also available. In addition, certain herbal formulas are showing promising results in the control of yeast overgrowth. Yeast has been proven to be sensitive to gentian formulas, garlic, caprylic acid, undecenoic acid, and rutin. (These treatments are still considered "experimental.") Along with antifungal medications, a diet which eliminates sugar, yeast, and many other foods is a critical part of the treatment. Symptoms may grow worse at the onset of treatment but may gradually improve if candida overgrowth is in fact contributing to the patient's problems.

Finally, it is important to note that *Candida albicans* is not the only yeast that may cause problems. Stool analysis may reveal various species of yeast. A yeast overgrowth of any kind may cause serious problems in various functions of the body. For example, minerals such as copper may not be properly absorbed. Also, since yeast overgrowths can interfere with the body's ability to regulate the absorption of essential fatty acids, it may be prudent to request an analysis of short- and long-chain fatty acid absorption when testing for yeast overgrowth by means of stool culture.

RESOURCES

American Academy of Environmental Medicine (AAEM)
#10 E Randolph St
New Hope, PA 18938
(215) 862-4544
May be able to refer you to a physician knowledgeable about candida overgrowth. Send self-addressed stamped envelope with request.

American Association of Naturopathic Physicians
601 Valley St, Suite 105
Seattle, WA 98109
(206) 298-0125
Can provide a list of naturopathic physicians or a referral to a registered physician in your area.

Autism Research Institute
4182 Adams Av
San Diego, CA 92116
(619) 281-7165
Can provide a "Candida Information and Questionnaire Packet" for $1. Packet includes candida questionnaire, newspaper articles on candida and autism, dietary guidelines, and an editorial by Bernard Rimland on the subject.

Critical Illness Research Foundation
2614 Highland Av
Birmingham, AL 35205
(205) 252-0855
Conducts research on *Candida albicans* and related problems. (Not an information service for parents.)

Great Plains Laboratory

9335 W 75th St
Overland Park, KS 66204
(913) 341-8949/(913) 341-6207 FAX
Dr. William Shaw, Director. Offers urine testing and treatment services for yeast overgrowth.

Great Smokies Diagnostic Laboratory

63 Zillicoa St
Asheville, NC 28801
(828) 253-0621
Can provide kit for stool analysis used for determining yeast overgrowth. Provides a very comprehensive profile of fatty acid absorption, and will also culture possible bacterial overgrowth. Can conduct sensitivity tests for the effects of antifungal drugs and "experimental" herbs on individual cultures.

Immuno Laboratories

1620 W Oakland Park Blvd
Ft. Lauderdale, FL 33311
(800) 476-4425
Dr. John Rebello, Director. A state, federal, and Medicare-licensed laboratory Immuno offers comprehensive diagnostic programs in the fields of allergy, immunology, and nutrition. Tests include IgG, IgE (food allergy blood tests) as well as Candida Albicans Assay.

International Health Foundation

PO Box 3494
Jackson, TN 38303-3494
(901) 660-7090
William G. Crook, MD, President; author of many books concerning children with allergies, yeast imbalances, and hyperactivity. Can provide information on health and learning problems related to yeast overgrowth.

SUGGESTED READING

Connolly, Pat. *The Candida Albicans Yeast-Free Cookbook*. New Canaan, CN: Keats Publishing, 1985.

Crook, William G. *Solving the Puzzle of Your Hard-To Raise Child*. New York: Random House, 1987.

———. *The Yeast Connection*. PO Box 3494, 681 Skyline Dr, Jackson, TN 38301: Professional Books, 1987.

Lorenzani, Shirley. *Candida: A Twentieth Century Disease*. New Canaan, CN: Keats Publishing, 1986.

Rapp, Doris. *Is This Your Child?* New York: William Morrow, 1991.

Rimland, Bernard. "Letter from the Autism Research Institute, Candida Packet" (original letter from Gus and Giana Mayo). San Diego: Autism Research Institute.

Trowbridge, John P., and Walker Morton. *The Yeast Syndrome*. New York: Bantam Books, 1986.

Truss, C. Orian. "Metabolic abnormalities in patients with chronic Candidiasis," *Journal of Orthomolecular Psychiatry*, vol. 13, no. 66, 1984.

Auditory Integration Training

Pioneered in France in the 1960's by Dr. Guy Berard, Auditory Integration Training (AIT) was introduced in the United States in 1990. AIT was brought to the attention of the general public in 1991 when Annabel Stehli's book, *The Sound of a Miracle: A Child's Triumph over Autism*, was published. Stehli's daughter, Georgie, who had been diagnosed with autism, eventually made dramatic improvements after receiving AIT.

Parents of children who have received AIT have noted a variety of improvements. Some feel it has made little difference in their child's behavior, while others have noted significant changes after their child received AIT. Some positive changes include increases in eye contact, spontaneous speech, socialization, and attention span, and a lessened sensitivity to certain sounds.

AIT is currently available throughout the United States and Canada, and there is growing evidence that many, but not all, children and adults with autism will benefit from this training. Drs. Bernard Rimland and Stephen Edelson have published two research studies on the efficiency of AIT and are completing two additional studies. In addition, many other researchers around the country are examining the effectiveness of AIT and are also obtaining positive results. These results include improvements in auditory processing and reductions in sound sensitivity and behavioral problems.

AIT includes a total of 10 hours of listening to modulated music over a 10-20 day period. Before receiving AIT the individual is given an audiogram, a test for hearing at various sound frequencies. According to Dr. Berard, a person might hear certain sound frequencies too well, and this may cause processing problems. In an audiogram, the frequencies which a person hears too well are referred to as "auditory peaks."

After the initial audiogram, the individual listens to music through a special machine by means of earphones. After five hours of listening, the individual is given another audiotest to see if auditory peaks are still present or if new ones have developed. Finally, a third audiotest is given at the end of the listening session to determine whether the individual's hearing has been normalized. [See Edelson et al.]

There are now two types of machines used in AIT: the Audiokinetron, developed by Dr. Berard in Annecy, France, and the BGC device developed by Bill Clark, an engineer in San Diego, California. The machines vary the music's sound, frequencies, and (BGC only) volume. Frequencies that an individual hears too well may be filtered out.

Experts are still not certain how or why AIT seems to reduce hearing hypersensitivity for some people. Theories suggest that AIT might reduce sound sensitivity either by eliminating peaks in hearing through filtration, by providing ear exercise, by massaging the inner ear and stimulating an acoustic reflex in the middle ear, by stimulating the brain, and/or by giving the person a chance to get used to loud sounds. The effectiveness of AIT may also lie in the sensory stimulation it provides to both the auditory system and the brain, and in reducing the distraction of background noise or noise in the ears. [See Fisher, pp. 4-5.]

Not all persons will benefit from AIT. However, many families continue to note improvements in their children after they have received the training. The improvement is usually subtle and may take several months to be noticed. Some individuals, after receiving AIT, may exhibit behavior problems that may last anywhere from two days to two months. Dr. Edelson encourages parents to employ consistent behavior management strategies during this adjustment period. [See Edelson and Waddell, p.4.] Often, positive gains in social, emotional, and academic development coincide with the difficult adjustment period. Continuing research will increase our understanding of this intervention.

RESOURCES

Autism Research Institute
4182 Adams Av
San Diego, CA 92116
(619) 281-7165
Dr. Bernard Rimland, Director. Can provide a list of practioners using the Audiokinetron and the BGC device. Will also send an information packet on Auditory Integration Training for $5.

Society for Auditory Integration Techniques
c/o Center for the Study of Autism
1040 Commercial St. SE
Salem, OR 97302
Dr. Stephen Edelson, President. The Society for Auditory Integration Techniques is dedicated to establishing guidelines, procedures, and ethics for AIT practitioners. Answers questions about AIT and research. Also distributes a quarterly newsletter. Membership is open to parents and professionals.

SUGGESTED READING

Berard, Guy. *Hearing Equals Behavior*. New Canaan, CT: Keats Publishing, 1982. Available through the Georgiana Organization and the Autism Research Institute.

Edelson, Stephen, and Lucinda Waddell. "Auditory Integration Training and the Auditory Training Project," Center for the Study of Autism Publication.

Fisher, Janine A. "Thank God we took a chance: Auditory training and Justin," *Outreach* (newsletter of the New Jersey Center for Outreach and Services for the Autism Community), vol. 8, no. 2, 1992, pp. 4-5, 10.

Rimland, B., and Edelson, S.M. "Auditory integration training: A pilot study," *Journal of Autism and Developmental Disorders*, vol. 25, 1995, pp. 61-70.

————."The effects of auditory integration training in autism," *American Journal of Speech-Language Pathology,* vol. 5, 1994, pp. 16-24.

Stehli, Annabel. *The Sound of a Miracle: A Child's Triumph over Autism.* New York: Doubleday, 1991.

Thivierge, J., C. Bedard, R. Cote, and M. Maziade. "Brainstem auditory evoked response and subcortical abnormalities in autism," *American Journal of Psychiatry*, 147, 1990, pp. 1609-1713.

Music Therapy

Individuals with autism have been treated with music therapy for many years now with varying degrees of success. Most popular in Europe, it is practiced worldwide. Music therapy seeks to use music as a facilitating agent, or therapeutic tool, to further growth and development in the client. Registered music therapists must undergo a college education, which includes courses in musicianship, behavioral and social sciences, as well as internship in a music therapy program. [See Boxhill, pp. 2-3.]

Music therapy in any individual case may include many activities, among them singing, movement to music, and playing instruments. Proponents of music therapy believe for a number of reasons that music can be used successfully as a medium for helping individuals with developmental disabilities, including autism. Among the reasons given are the following:

• **Music therapy requires no verbal interaction** although it may eventually facilitate it.

- **By nature, music is structured**, and it can facilitate structure in the environment in which it is experienced. Sound stimulus can aide in sensory integration because it involves all the senses. The vestibular system is also stimulated when rhythmic movement is included in the therapy.

- **Music naturally facilitates play** and therefore enhances learning through play.

- **Music therapy can aid in socialization and influence behavior.**

In general, music therapists hope to improve various aspects of a client's physical and mental health and to foster desired changes in behavior. A qualified music therapist makes a careful assessment of the individual's present capabilities and, on that basis, defines program goals, both long- and short-term. Music therapy can be carried out in a private setting, but it can also be incorporated into a child's program at school. [See Lathom.] An interested parent could also learn techniques for using music as a teaching tool at home. [See Meilahn, pp. 19-20.]

RESOURCES

National Association of Music Therapy (NAMT)
8455 Colesville Rd, Suite 1000
Silver Spring, MD 20910
(301) 589-3300
Founded in 1950. Aims to establish qualifications and standards of training for music therapists. Maintains placement services. Will send information on particular topics on request.

The Nordoff-Robbins Music Therapy Centre
2 Lissenden Gardens
London NW5 IPP
United Kingdom
071-267-4496
Offers private and group music therapy classes for individuals with autism and other disabilities.

REI Institute
HC 75 Box 420
Lamy, NM 87540
(800) 659-6644
www.reiinstitute.com
Jeff Strong, President. Developed by Jeff Strong, Rhythmic Entrainment Intervention™ (REI) is a therapy program that applies specific sensory input to the nervous system through the use of recorded drum rhythms. The foundation of REI's theory is that specialized rhythms can alter the physiological functioning of the body and improve the functioning of the brain. Research information available on request. Offers several program options, from custom-made recordings to generalized relaxation tapes, developed for individuals with neurological conditions such as autism, ADHD, and chronic pain.

SUGGESTED READING

Alvin, Julliette and Warwick, Auriel. *Music Therapy for the Autistic Child.* New York: Oxford University Press, 1991.

Boxhill, Edith Hillman. *Music Therapy for the Developmentally Disabled.* Rockville, MD: Aspen Publishers, 1985.

——. Music Therapy for Living: *The Principle of Normalization Embodied in Music Therapy.* St. Louis, MO: MMB

Bruscia, Kenneth E. *Defining Music Therapy*. Phoenixville, PA: Barcelona Publishers, 1989.

Croall, Jonathan. "The Sound of Silence," *The London Times Educational Supplement*, Sept. 20, 1991.

Davis, William B., Gfeller, Kate and Thaut, Michail H. *An Introduction to Music Therapy: Theory and Practice*. Dubuque, IA: William C. Brown Publishers, 1992.

Lathom, Wanda. *The Role of Music Therapy in the Education of Handicapped Children and Youth*, Report of The National Association for Music Therapy. Lawrence, KS, 1980.

Meilahn, Daniel C. "Music and the autistic child: A family affair," *The Advocate*, vol. 18, no. 5, 1986, pp.19-20.

Nordoff, Paul, and Clive Robbins. *Music Therapy in Special Education*. New York: John Day, 1971.

——. *Creative Music Therapy*. New York: John Day, 1976.

Peters, Jacqueline Schmidt. *Music Therapy: An Introduction*. Springfield, IL: Charles C. Thomas, 1987.

Schalkwijk, F.W. *Music and People with Developmental Disabilities: Music Therapy, Remedial Music Making and Musical Activities*. Bristol, PA: Jessica Kingsley Publishers, 1994.

Schulberg, Cecilia H. *The Music Therapy Sourcebook*. New York: Human Sciences Press, 1981.

Streeter, Elaine. Making Music with the Young Child with Special Needs. Bristol, PA: Jessica Kingsley Publishers, 1993.

Doman/Delacato Method

The 1960s gave us breakthroughs in the treatment of children with brain injuries that have also had great impact on the diagnosis and treatment of children with autism. Two important contributors to this field are Glenn Doman and Carl Delacato. Doman's book, *What to Do About Your Brain-Injured Child*, and Delacato's book, *The Ultimate Stranger*, although both written in 1974, are still important sources of information on the neurological aspects of the person with autism.

The Institute for the Achievement of Human Potential in Philadelphia was founded in the early 1960s by Glenn Doman, Robert Doman, and Carl Delacato. They had been working with children with brain injuries since the early 1950s with the neurosurgeon, Dr. Temple Fay, at his Neurological Rehabilitation Center, also in Philadelphia.

Years of research led the team to conclude that there were many forms of brain injury, the form depending on the area of the brain affected and the extent of the damage. In children with brain injuries, sensory information is interrupted in some way and does not get properly routed to the various centers of the brain. Departing from the theories of that time, which approached brain injury from an all-or-nothing standpoint and considered it incurable, the Institute labeled children according to their brain organization:

• **Mild.** Suffering from perceptual problems (how the world is perceived via the senses).

• **Moderate.** Able to move and make sounds; detectable by medical testing.

• **Severe.** Unable to move or make sounds, obvious lack of bodily functions. [Delacato, *The Ultimate Stranger*.]

Doman and Delacato believed that such damage may be caused by lack of oxygen during the birth process, by a high fever during the early period of the child's brain development, or for other reasons. While there was much controversy about their methods of identification and treatment, the term "minimal brain injury" eventually came into vogue. Unfortunately, it became a catch-all instead of an accurate diagnosis and often did not lead to proper treatment.

Their research led them to conclude that, in order for children to reach their full potential, certain natural stages of development must occur. To evaluate each stage, they tested six major areas of development: vision, hearing, tactility, mobility, function of the hands and feet, and language. They maintained that a child could not skip one stage and be expected to achieve full potential in the following stages. For example, research showed that many children with reading difficulties lack coordination skills. Even though they show no signs of brain damage, they have for some reason skipped a critical developmental stage, such as crawling, which provides stimulation to those parts of the brain in which visual perception is coordinated.

The Doman/Delacato theory holds that the brain can develop only if it is used. In order to develop properly, it must receive the necessary stimulation. To treat children or adults brought to them for help, they devised ways to let them reexperience these normal stages of development by stimulating the brain through movement of the body. For instance, if children could not walk well, they gave them the opportunity to learn to crawl. The widely known term, "patterning," refers to the manipulation of someone's body in imitation of creeping or crawling movements when the person is unable to make the movements on their own.

Today, unfortunately, the term patterning still conjures up the vision of a 14-hour marathon of volunteers working with a child. Unless there is a truly severe injury, new techniques often require no more than an hour or two of organized programming per day.

Carl Delacato

In 1963, the Institute for the Achievement of Human Potential assigned Carl Delacato the task of researching problems of human behavior. At that time, behavior was beginning to be seen as a reflection of the function—or dysfunction—of the nervous system. He chose to study children with autism because, in his opinion, their behavior disorders were the most complex and difficult to treat. He believed that the sometimes "bizarre" behaviors, such as spinning, slapping, or feces smearing, might somehow be a means of coping with an internal sensory awareness that is somehow very different from the sensory system of a "normal" body. He felt that children with autism were like the children with brain injuries he had treated successfully before.

Delacato went on to classify the areas in which sensory input was not normal. He called the ways in which children dealt with these often terrifying sensations, "sensoryisms." One example of a sensoryism, which he called "hyper-vision," would be a child who stares for hours at a time at a drop of saliva or at specks of dust. Any of the five senses—vision, hearing, tactility, smell, and taste—may be affected. Delacato diagnosed these distortions as hypersensitivity, hyposensitivity, and white noise. "Hyper" refers to too much stimulus entering the nervous system, "hypo" refers to too little, and, finally, "white noise" refers to a kind of internal static that disrupts input from external stimuli. Careful observation of each child helped Delacato determine which sensory systems had gone awry.

Methods were developed to decrease or increase stimulus input, depending on the child's individual needs. After the sensory system was "normalized" to the point at which the child could tolerate the sensations coming toward him or her, Delacato would treat the child much as he did other children with brain injury. Delacato was honest enough to state that not all the children he treated could be reached or helped by him. After several years of treatment, however, many showed great improvement. Delacato and his associates continue to help children with autism and other people with varying degrees of brain injury. Most of the treatment was then, and is today, carried out in home programs by the parents. His methods today incorporate the many changes developed over the years, such as nutritional regimens, reflex stimulation, cranial manipulation where indicated, and simple methods of behavior management. *The Ultimate Stranger* is still an excellent resource for anyone wishing to learn more about the details of this method.

RESOURCES

American Academy for Human Development
850 South Main
Piqua, OH 45356
Comprised of members from varied disciplines who have a commitment to work with individuals who are functioning inefficiently because of a lack of neurological organization. Can provide a list of centers that work with people with brain injuries.

Center for Neurological Rehabilitation
32 South Morton Av
Morton, PN 19070
(610) 544-6610 /(210) 722-2411 (Texas Center)
John Unruh, Director. Rehabilitation center for those with brain injuries.

Delacato and Delacato
Consultants in Learning
Suite 107, Plymouth Plaza
Plymouth Meeting, PA 19462
(610) 828-4881
Carl Delacato and Robert Delacato, Directors. Can provide information on international centers. Works with children with brain injuries and autism.

The Institute For the Achievement of Human Potential
8801 Stenton Av
Wyndmoor, PA 19038
(215) 233-2050
Glenn Doman, Director. Works with individuals with brain injury. Can provide a list of affiliated institutes.

Fern Ridge Press

1927 McLean Blvd
Eugene, OR 97405
Distributes a series of video-tapes concerning neuro-developmental intervention, produced in conjunction with Peter Blythe of the Institute of Neuro-Physiological Psychology of London, England.

Northwest Neurodevelopmental Training Center

PO Box 406
152 Arthur St
Woodburn, OR 97071
(503) 981-0635
Susan Scott, Director. Works with children with brain injuries and autism.

Springall Academy

6550 Soledad Mountain Rd
LaJolla, CA 92037
(619) 459-9047
Peter Springall, Director. Formerly the San Diego Academy for Neurological Development. Works with brain-injured individuals and individuals with autism.

SUGGESTED READING

Delacato, Carl. *The Ultimate Stranger*. New York: Doubleday, 1974, 1984.

———. *A New Start for the Child with Reading Problems*. New York: David McKay, 1981.

Doman, Glenn. *What to Do About Your Brain-Injured Child*. New York: Doubleday, 1974, 1990.

———. *How to Teach Your Baby to Read*. New York: Doubleday, 1975.

Gold, Svea. *When Children Invite Child Abuse*. Eugene, OR: Fern Ridge Press,1986.

Melton, David. *Todd*. Englewood Cliffs, NJ: Prentice-Hall, 1968.

Osteopathy/ Craniosacral Therapy[SM]

Dr. John E. Upledger, an osteopathic physician and surgeon, developed a light-touch, manipulative therapy, termed "craniosacral therapy" in the early 1970s. Osteopathy is a similar therapy in which gentle manipulation is given to various parts of the body to free restrictions of motion. Both osteopathy and craniosacral therapy are practiced by health practitioners worldwide.

Some of Upledger's techniques are based on the work of Dr. William Sutherland, whose work, known as "cranial osteopathy," involves manipulation of the bones of the cranium. Sutherland believed the bones in the skull evolved to provide opportunity for movement and that, when their movement becomes restricted for various reasons, head pains, coordination difficulties, and other problems may occur.

In 1975, Upledger and other scientists at Michigan State University's College of Osteopathic Medicine investigated Sutherland's theory that skull bones move in response to hydraulic pressure of cerebrospinal fluid. The team concluded that the skull's sutures are not hardened structures, but are elastic, containing nerve fibers, blood vessels, and elastic tissue.

Upledger refined his work on the bones of the skull, face, and mouth (cranium) to include the bones from the spinal cord down to the sacrum and coccyx, all of which he includes in the craniosacral system. He also views the brain and spinal cord as connected by a hydraulic system encased in three tough membranes which are separated from one another by fluid-filled spaces. According to Upledger, movement of the fluid up and down the spinal cord creates movement in the membranes which, in turn, affects connective tissue in the body. An imbalance in the craniosacral system can affect the development of the brain and spinal cord, which can result in various bodily dysfunctions. Craniosacral therapy provides a way to examine movements in the various parts of the system and to free them from restrictions by means of gentle pressure from the therapist.

Upledger has conducted studies on children with autism to determine if there is any correlation between restrictions in this population. He believes children who are considered "classically autistic" in behavioral terms show similar patterns of restriction in the craniosacral system. [See Upledger and Vredevoogd, pp. 262-64.] According to Upledger and in anecdotal reports from parents, improvements in behaviors such as head-banging and wrist-biting have been noted in children after they received craniosacral therapy. Also reported are improvements in communication and lessening of hyperactivity. With further research in this field, the effectiveness of this treatment for autism may be further substantiated.

RESOURCES

The Cranial Academy
8202 Clearvista Pkwy, Suite 9D
Indianapolis, IN 46256
(317) 594-0411
Offers a patient brochure on osteopathy. Provides a list of practitioners who have undergone a minimum of 40 hours of special training in cranial manipulation.

Osteopathic Centre for Children
4 Harcourt House
19a Cavendish Square
London, UK WIM 9AD
071-495 1231.
A Registered Charity whose clinic staff treat children with many disabilities, including autism. Treatment is based on the work of William Sutherland and others.

Neuro Therapeutics
PO Box 1126/921 Seventh St
Oregon City, OR 97045
(503) 657-8903
Karen Brelje, Director. Specializing in the treatment of children with nervous system disorders. Offers craniosacral therapy as part of a holistic treatment approach.

The Upledger Institute
11211 Prosperity Farm Rd, Suite 325
Palm Beach Gardens, FL 33410-3487
(800) 233-5880 or (561) 622-4334
Works with individuals and offers information on the work of Dr. Upledger. Also trains practitioners in the use of craniosacral therapy. Can refer you to a practitioner in your area.

SUGGESTED READING

Reuben, Carolyn. "Craniosacral therapy: Adjusting the bones in the skull can affect the way you feel and act," *East/West*, Oct. 1987, pp. 22-25.

The Upledger Institute. "Discover the CranioSacral System," Palm Beach Gardens, FL, 1988.

Upledger, John E. "Craniosacral function in brain dysfunction," *Osteopathic Annals*, vol. 11, no. 7, 1983, pp. 318-24.

Upledger, John E., and Jon D. Vredevoogd. *Craniosacral Therapy*. Seattle: Eastland Press, 1983.

Sensory Integration Therapy

Dr. Jean Ayers pioneered the theory that some children suffer from a neural disorder that causes the nervous system to receive incoming information, via the senses, in an inefficient manner. This disturbance, called Sensory Integrative Disorder (SID), may be present in some individuals with autism.

Besides the obvious senses of sight, taste, touch, smell, and hearing, our nervous system also senses pressure, movement, body position, and the force of gravity. These senses are known as tactile (touch), vestibular (movement), and proprioceptive (body position). The tactile, vestibular, and proprioceptive systems work closely with other systems in our body and help us make appropriate responses to incoming sensations and to our environment. Sensory integration (SI) is the term used to define this complex process.

When sensory integration does not develop normally in a child, a number of difficulties may arise. Indicators of sensory integrative dysfunction may include:

- **oversensitivity to touch, movements, sights, or sounds**

- **underreaction to sensory stimulation**

- **unusually high or low levels of activity**

- **coordination problems**

- **delays in speech, language, and motor skills**

- **behavior problems**

- **poor self concept.**

If sensory integrative problems are suspected, a child can be evaluated by a physical or occupational therapist who has received certification in SI therapy. For a list of qualified professionals, contact Sensory Integration International (address listed below). Often insurance policies will partially cover physical or occupational therapy. Also, there may be a therapist employed by your school district who has received SI certification. Even if your child is not attending school, he or she may qualify for their services.

Sensory integrative therapy (SIT) is highly individualized, with activities designed to meet the child's unique developmental needs. A very important component of SIT is that the therapist pays close attention to what motivates the child. Most children will be drawn to the activities that benefit them the most. If the child has difficulty choosing activities, the therapist provides more structure. Because SIT resembles play, most children enjoy it. Equipment may include swings, bolsters, slides, and scooterboards, and materials for fine motor activities are also available.

Successful therapy will increase the child's ability to

integrate sensory information efficiently. Improvements in motor coordination, language development, reduction of "hyper" or "hypo" responsiveness to sensory stimuli, better emotional adjustment, and self-confidence are possible benefits. Careful monitoring and documentation of your child's development should be conducted by the therapist. Treatment may last from six months to two years, depending on the unique needs of the child.

RESOURCES

The American Occupational Therapy Association (AOTA)
4720 Montgomery Ln
PO Box 31220
Bethesda, MD 20824-1220
(301) 652-2682
National organization of occupational therapists. Can provide listings of therapists in your region.

Center for Neurodevelopmental Studies
5430 West Glenn Dr
Glendale, AZ 85301
(602) 915-0345
Makes available information on sensory integrative therapy. Packet of articles and bibliography, $7.50.

Developmental Concepts
PO Box 31759
Phoenix, AZ 85046-1759
(888) 287-3239/ (602) 482-9851 FAX
E-mail: atready@bitstream.net
Website: www.developmentalconcepts.com
Bonnie Hanschu, Director. Offers seminars, publications, products, and a newsletter related to sensory processing disorders. Offers a two day course which compares autism and

attention deficit disorder from a sensory perspective. Hanschu is the creator of the Ready Approach, an organized approach that emphasizes integrated, recurring, doses of brainstem sensation embedded in the natural routine for people who have autism or related disorders.

North American Riding for the Handicapped Association
(Therapeutic Horseback Riding)
(800) 369-RIDE
An association of accredited therapeutic horseback instructors who work with occupational therapists to provide sensory therapy through horseback riding for individuals with disabilities.

Sensory Integration International (SII)
1602 Cabrillo Av
Torrance, CA 90501-2819
(310) 320-9986
A nonprofit organization that provides general information on sensory integration and information on specific subjects. Can also provide a list of occupational and physical therapists who have been certified in sensory integrative therapy.

SUGGESTED READING

Ayres, A. Jean. *Sensory Integration and the Child.* Los Angeles: Western Psychological Services, 1979.

Ayres, A. J., and L.S. Tickle. "Hyper-responsivity to touch and vestibular stimuli as a predictor of positive response to sensory integration procedures by autistic children," *American Journal of Occupational Therapy*, vol. 34, 1980, pp. 375-86.

Hutchinson, Carol. "Interview with Lorna Jean King," *The Advocate*, vol. 27, no. 5, 1995, pp.18-19.

King, L.J. "Sensory integration: An effective approach to therapy and education," *Autism Research Review International*, vol. 5, no. 2, 1991, pp. 3, 6.

Merrill, Susan Cook [ed.]. *Environment: Implications for Occupational Therapy Practice, A Sensory Integrative Perspective*. Rockville, MD: The American Occupational Therapy Association, 1990.

Sensory Integration International. *A Parents' Guide To Sensory Integration*. Torrance, CA, 1991.

Sensory Integration Quarterly. Newsletter on SI and related subjects for therapists, parents, and teachers. Distributed through Sensory Integration International.

Trot, Maryann, Marcie K. Laurel, and Susan L. Windich. *Sensabilities: Understanding Sensory Integration*. 1993. (Available from Therapy Skill Builders, PO Box 42050, Tucson, AZ 85733.)

Video:
Reisman, Judith and Lorna Jean King. *Making Contact: Sensory Integration and Autism.* (Available from Media Learning Systems, Continuing Education Programs of America, PO Box 52, Peoria, IL 61650, (309) 263-0310.)

The Squeeze Machine

Many individuals with autism show tactile defensiveness and a reluctance to be held. The squeeze machine is a device used to give deep pressure stimulation, which may have a calming effect on some individuals with autism and increase their tolerance for human touch. The squeeze machine was invented by Dr. Temple Grandin, a woman with autism who is now an assistant professor at Colorado State University. She is considered one of the foremost experts in the design and construction of livestock handling facilities.

In her book, *Emergence: Labeled Autistic*, Grandin describes her desire as a young child for deep pressure stimulation, but how she also felt overwhelmed by the sensory stimulation of an embrace. She writes that as a five-year old she would dream of a machine that could apply the comforting pressure she longed for. In her teens, Grandin visited her aunt's ranch, where she noticed cattle would sometimes relax when pressure was applied to them in a squeeze chute. She decided to try the cattle chute herself and found that it offered her relief from nervousness and anxiety. At age 18 she built a prototype squeeze machine and successfully used it to reduce her tactile defensiveness. After she gradually learned to tolerate being held by the machine, she was able to tolerate being touched or hugged by people.

Over the years Dr. Grandin perfected the squeeze machine. It is a fully padded, V-shaped device that is designed to apply pressure over most of the body. The user of the machine is in complete control and can adjust the amount of pressure the machine applies. Pressure is controlled by a lever-operated pneumatic valve, which is connected to an air cylinder that pulls the side boards together. The pressure remains constant, even when the user shifts position. [See Grandin, "Calming effects...," p. 65.]

It is interesting to note that Dr. Grandin began her designing career with livestock handling equipment as the result of channeling her intense interest or "fixation" with cattle chutes and the squeeze machine. A caring, compassionate teacher encouraged her to learn all she could about *why* the machine had a calming effect. Because she was so interested in this, she eventually chose a career in animal science. Grandin believes that fixations can serve as motivators for learning. Instead of trying to stamp out a child's narrow interest, she encourages parents and teachers to broaden those interests into constructive activities. For instance, she suggests, that if a child is interested in vacuum cleaners, an instructional manual for vacuums might make an engaging textbook for that child. Grandin writes that if she had not been encouraged to develop and understand her fixation with the squeeze machine she "might be sitting somewhere rotting in front of a TV instead of writing this chapter." [Grandin, in Schopler et al., p. 115.]

Although there is a lack of formal research data on the effectiveness of the squeeze machine, some studies have concluded that the squeeze machine reduces hyperactivity and tactile defensiveness in some children with autism. [See Imamura et al.] Anecdotal reports suggest that the squeeze machine may be a beneficial component of sensory integrative therapy. Grandin states, "... the squeeze machine should be considered a novel treatment that has not been subjected to careful evaluation of clinical efficacy or safety." [Grandin, "Calming effects...," p.70.] However, the machine is now commercially available.

RESOURCES

Therafin Corporation
19747 Wolf Rd
Mokena, IL 60448
(708) 479-7300
Manufactures and markets the squeeze machine. Write or call for information and price.

Center for Neurodevelopmental Studies
5430 West Glenn Dr
Glendale, AZ 85301
(602) 915-0345
Lorna King, Director. Can provide information on sensory integrative therapy. The center has used the squeeze machine in a sensory integrative program for children with autism and children with hyperactive behavior.

SUGGESTED READING

Grandin, Temple. *Thinking in Pictures: And Other Reports from My Life with Autism.* New York: Doubleday, 1995.

Grandin, Temple, and Margaret Scariano. *Emergence: Labeled Autistic.* Arena Press, 20 Commercial Blvd, Novato, CA: 1986 (updated 1989).

———. "Calming effects of deep touch pressure in patients with autistic disorder, college students, and animals," *Journal of Child and Adolescent Psychopharmacology,* vol. 2, no. 1, 1992.

———. "An Inside View of Autism," in *High-Functioning Individuals with Autism.* Schopler, Eric, and Gary Mesibov [eds.]. New York: Plenum Press, 1992.

Imamura, K.N., T. Wiess, and D. Parham. "The effects of hug machine usage on behavioral organization of children with autism and autistic-like characteristics," *Sensory Integration Quarterly,* vol. 27, 1990, pp. 1-5.

Holding Therapy

Holding therapy gained widespread attention when Dr. Martha Welch, a child psychiatrist from New York, began using it as a means of working with children with autism in the late 1970s. She has written about her work in the book, *Holding Time*. Holding therapy has many advocates who claim remarkable results, as well as many detractors who disagree with its intrusive nature as well as with some of the theories as to why it may be effective.

During holding therapy the parent attempts to make contact with the child in various ways. This may mean simply comforting a distressed child. But often the parent may hold the child for extended periods of time even if the child is fighting heavily against the embrace. The child sits or lies face-to-face with the parent, who continually tries to establish eye contact, as well as to share feelings verbally throughout the holding session. Holding is often done when the child is crying, screaming or showing signs of distress. The parent remains calm and in control and offers comfort when the child stops resisting. Holding can be as short as a few minutes, but it can also last for hours at a time.

Much of the controversy surrounding holding therapy stems from the idea that holding increases mother-child bonding. Dr. Welch is a firm believer that it is the child's mother who should do the holding. Some proponents theorize that because the bonding process between the parent and child has not had adequate opportunity to develop, the child may as a result feel the emotions of fear and isolation. Holding therapy attempts to break down this isolation and premature emotional independence by insisting on communication through physical contact. Some advocates point out that there is no *blaming* of the mother for the child's behavior, but that the mother can play an integral role in the child's recovery.

Skeptics of the bonding theory believe that holding therapy may work in some cases by decreasing tactile defensiveness in a child with autism and may thus be a more stressful version of sensory integration therapy. [See Grandin, p. 6.] Children with autism often suffer from a sensory system that does not properly process sensory input and vestibular (the sensory system in the inner ear) stimulation. Other researchers theorize that holding may somehow help stimulate parts of the brain, such as the cerebellum, where sensory input is processed. [See Rimland, p. 3.] Brain studies have noted abnormalities in the cerebellum in some individuals with autism.

Controversy continues over why and how different forms of holding therapy work. Some researchers have used holding as a negative reinforcer. An increase in eye contact and tolerance of physical contact was noted when one child was subjected to holding sessions with a trainer and was rewarded when his crying lessened. Gradually, the amount of holding time required to earn free time was increased. After nine 90-minute sessions, the child was able to tolerate the holding without screaming, and other benefits were noted as well. [See Powers et al.]

It is interesting to note that a form of holding therapy is also gaining popularity with some therapists as a means of reaching children who do not have autism but suffer from what is known as "attachment disorders." These children have often suffered from severe abuse and/or neglect and have become extremely antisocial and sometimes a danger to themselves and their caretakers. The work with these children is based on the work of Robert Zaslow, an analyst who in the 1960s developed a type of holding therapy known as "rage reduction therapy," which he used for children with autism. [See Keogh, p. 53.]

Holding therapy as a means to treat autism will undoubtedly continue to have its supporters. Parents have formed "mothering centers" which serve as support groups for parents using holding therapy with their children. Hopefully, scientific research will continue to answer many of the still unresolved questions regarding how, why, and if, holding therapy may be effective for some children with autism.

RESOURCES
Dr. Martha Welch/The Mothering Center
235 Cognewaugh Rd
Cos Cob, CN 06807
(203) 661-1413
Dr. Welch is one of the foremost advocates of holding therapy in the US. She has private practices in both Connecticut and New York City.

The National Autistic Society (United Kingdom)
276 Willesden Lane
London, NW2 5RB
United Kingdom
The National Autistic Society's publication, *Communication*, has covered the topic of holding therapy in several issues. The Welch holding method is widely used in Europe.

The Tinbergen Trust/The Mothering Centre
8 Somerset Road
Teddington, Middlesex, TW11 8RS
United Kingdom
Contact Mrs. Jasmine Bayley. The Tinbergen Trust was established to provide support to both parents and professionals using holding techniques.

SUGGESTED READING

Grandin, Temple. "An autistic person's view of holding therapy," *The Advocate*, vol. 22, no. 4, 1990-91, pp. 6-8.

Keogh, Tom. "Children without a conscience," *New Age Journal*, Jan./Feb. 1993, pp. 53-57, 128-30.

Mason, Janet. "Child of silence: Retrieved from the shadow world of autism, Katy finds her voice," *Life Magazine*, vol. 10, Sept. 1987, pp. 84-89.

Maurice, Catherine. *Let Me Hear Your Voice*. New York: Alfred Knopf, 1993.

Powers, Michael D., and Carolyn A. Thorwarth. "The effect of negative reinforcement on tolerance of physical contact in a preschool autistic child," *Journal of Clinical Psychology*, vol. 14, no. 4, 1985, pp. 299-303. [Reviewed in *Autism Research Review International*, vol. 1, no. 1, 1987, p. 5.]

Rimland, Bernard. "Holding therapy: Maternal bonding or cerebellar stimulation?" *Autism Research Review International*, vol. 1, no. 3, 1987, p. 3.

Tinbergen, Niko, and Elizabeth A. Tinbergen. *Autistic Children: New Hope for a Cure*. London: Allen and Unwin, 1983.

Welch, Martha. *Holding Time*. London: Century Hutchinson, 1989.

The Son-Rise Program®
(As taught at The Option Institute and Fellowship)

Barry Neil and Samahria Kaufman, founders of The Option Institute and Fellowship, pioneered their own method of working with children with autism in the early 1970s, when they successfully helped their son, Raun, fully recover from autism using an intensive, one-on-one approach.

In his book *Son-Rise: The Miracle Continues*, Barry Kaufman describes his son as exhibiting many of the characteristics of autism, such as appearing deaf at times, fascination with inanimate objects, aloofness, rocking, self-stimulatory behavior, and marked lack of communication skills, both verbal and nonverbal. At eighteen months, Raun was formally diagnosed as autistic and functionally retarded by psychiatric and developmental professionals. [See Option Institute, "Family Programs for Special

Children."] After searching nationwide without finding a program that would offer hope for Raun's recovery, the Kaufmans decided to try to help him on their own. They designed an intensive stimulation program based on an attitude of unconditional love and acceptance. After three years of this home-based, parent-directed program, Raun completely emerged from his condition with no signs of autism.

The book *Son-Rise*, which was also made into an NBC-TV movie, is scheduled to be republished in 1994 with a revised section chronicling their three-year program with Raun and updating the boy's development through age 20. An additional new section of the book tells the stories of other families who have used the Son-Rise Program to help their children. The book *A Miracle to Believe In*, also by Kaufman, tells the story of the Kaufmans' work with another boy with severe autism. Although this child did not recover from autism, he showed significant improvement after a year and a half of intensive intervention by the Kaufmans and the child's parents.

The Son-Rise Program, based on a loving, non-judgmental attitude, encourages following the child's lead or actions while simultaneously motivating him or her to expand his/her world. Special emphasis is placed on trusting and respecting the child. High-energy play sessions in an environment geared specifically for a child with autism are also features of a home-based Son-Rise Program. The central idea is that the child will be motivated to find ways to reach out to parents and volunteers trained to present a consistent attitude of acceptance and enthusiasm.

As a result of great demand from parents wishing to learn more about this method, the Kaufmans founded The Option Institute and Fellowship (a nonprofit organization) in Sheffield, Mass. in 1983. The Institute offers training for families wishing to create home-based Son-Rise Programs for their special children. The Son-Rise Programs at the Option Institute are *highly individualized* and last from one week to a month or more.

The unique feature of the Son-Rise Program, as taught by the Kaufmans and the staff at the Option Institute, is the foremost commitment to happiness. By using a gentle, non-directive approach known as The Optiva Dialogue[SM], parents are first encouraged to explore their beliefs about themselves and their situation. These dialogue sessions provide a time and place to question judgments that are limiting and to affirm the power of a truly loving and accepting attitude. Personal Optiva Dialogue sessions play a major role in the Son-Rise Program both at the Institute and in home-based programs run by parents trained at the Institute. Parents are encouraged to continue using these skills to explore their beliefs and to become the most loving and accepting teachers they can be for themselves and their special child.

During a typical stay at the Institute, parents observe the staff working with their child. They are also given opportunities to work with their child using the Son-Rise Program, after which they receive feedback from the staff. Parent training also includes defining base lines, observing behavior, documenting progress, and developing program strategies for working with the individual child. Because of the time-intensive work typical of a Son-Rise home program, parents are encouraged to recruit volunteers to help them work with their child. During their stay at the Institute, parents are given advice on how to carefully recruit, train, and monitor the work of volunteers in their program. For families who have established home Son-Rise Programs for their children, the Institute offers outreach and support services as well as Advanced Family Training Workshops.

At present, no formal studies or evaluations have validated the effectiveness of the Son-Rise Program as a treatment for children with autism. The program requires immense commitment and dedication on the part of the child's family, and for some parents this has proved to be more demanding and rigorous than they are able to maintain. Parents wishing to explore this program are encouraged to read the literature and contact the Institute's staff for detailed information.

RESOURCE
The Option Institute and Fellowship
2080 South Undermountain Rd
Sheffield, MA 01257
(413) 229-2100/(413) 229-8931 FAX
The Option Institute offers many books and tapes that explain the Kaufmans' philosophy and methods of working with special children, as well as other books about the Option Process®. Free catalog of workshops and programs for special children. Special Children/Special Solutions, a four-tape audio set, is a helpful question-and-answer session with Samahria Kaufman in which she discusses home-based programs and answers commonly asked questions about the Option Institute's methods of working with special children. The Institute also loans the movie, *Son-Rise*, with a refundable deposit.

SUGGESTED READING

Kaufman, Barry Neil. *Son-Rise: The Miracle Continues.* Tiburon, CA: H.J. Kramer, 1994

———. *To Love is To Be Happy With.* New York: Ballantine Books, 1977.

———. *Giant Steps.* New York: Ballantine Books, Random House, 1979.

———. *A Miracle To Believe In.* New York: Ballantine Books, Random House, 1981.

———. *Happiness Is A Choice.* New York: Ballantine Books, Random House, 1991.

The Option Institute and Fellowship. "The Son-Rise Program®," Sheffield, MA, 1993.

Appendix

Association for Comprehensive NeuroTherapy
1128 Royal Palm Beach Blvd, #283
Royal Palm Beach, FL 33411
(561) 798-0472
http://www.latitudes.org
Publishes the newsletter, *Latitudes*. Membership includes referrals to alternative therapists, list of national organizations and newsletter subscription.

The Association for Persons with Severe Handicaps (TASH)
29 W Susquehanna Av, Suite 210
Baltimore, MD 21204
(410) 828-TASH
An organization of parents and professionals working for the rights of all people with severe handicaps. Publishes a newsletter and a professional journal which include topics concerning autism.

Association for Retarded Citizens (ARC)

500 E Border St, Suite 300
Arlington, TX 76010
(817) 261-6003

Coordinates a network of local chapters. Provides information and advocacy. Local chapters may offer respite care programs and other opportunities for persons with severe disabilities.

Autism Directory Service

106 Freedom Plains Rd, Suite 191
Poughkeepsie, NY 12603

Offers general information and referral services. Publishes quarterly newsletter, *The Facilitator.*

Autism Network for Hearing or Visually Impaired Persons

7510 Oceanfront Av
Virginia Beach, VA 23451
(757) 428-9036

Dolores and Alan Bartel, Organizers. The network serves as a data bank of families, professionals, and others interested in education, research, and advocacy for those with autism and other sensory disabilities.

Autism Research Institute (ARI)

4182 Adams Av
San Diego, CA 92116
(619) 281-7165

Dr. Bernard Rimland, Director. An information-sharing network for parents and professionals. A priority of the Institute is evaluating the various treatments used to help people with autism. Dr. Rimland is one of the leading scientists in the field of biomedical research on autism. Publishes the quarterly newsletter, *Autism Research Review International.*

Autism Resource Network

5123 Westmill Rd
Minnetonka, MN 55345
(612) 988-0088/(612) 988-0099 FAX

Cherri Saltzman, Director. A nonprofit organization offering books as well as other products related to autism. The network publishes a quarterly newsletter available for $15 per year.

Autism Services Center/National Autism Hotline

Prichard Bldg
605 9th St
Huntington, WV 25710-0507
(304) 525-8014

The Autism Hotline is a free service. The Center provides information, as well as advocacy and consulting services for those involved with autistic people.

Autism Society of America (ASA)

7910 Woodmont Av, Suite 650
Bethesda, MD 20814
(301) 657-0881/(800) 3AUTISM

A national support group for parents and professionals. Publishes the magazine, *The Advocate*, free with membership. The ASA Information and Referral Service offers information on autism and services for people with autism. Coordinates a network of affiliated local chapters.

Autism Society of Michigan Bookstore

6035 Executive Dr, Suite 109
Lansing, MI 48911
(517) 882-2800

Offers an extensive selection of books and materials concerning autism and other disability issues.

Autism Society of North Carolina Bookstore

505 Oberlin Rd, Suite 230
Raleigh, NC 27605-1345
(919) 743-0204
Can provide over 90 different titles on autism and related topics. Purchase orders from school systems and nonprofit organizations are accepted.

Bittersweet Farms

12660 Archbold-Whitehouse Rd
Whitehouse, OH 43571
(419) 875-6986
A farm community for people with autism. Can provide information on the Bittersweet Farm model.

Children's Defense Fund

25 East St, NW
Washington, D.C. 20001
(202) 628-8339
A legal organization working to expand the rights of children. Efforts include lobbying and bringing cases to court.

COSAC/ The Autism Helpline

1450 Parkside Av, Suite 22
Ewing, NJ 08638
(609) 883-8100/(800) 4-AUTISM (in NJ)
COSAC stands for The New Jersey Center for Outreach and Services for the Autism Community and primarily serves the residents of New Jersey. However, out-of-state residents may request information about services for the autistic community through the Autism Helpline and Information Clearinghouse.

Council For Exceptional Children
1920 Association Dr
Reston, VA 20191-1589
(703) 620-3660
Committed to improving educational outcomes for individuals with exceptionalities. Provides access to an international library and database specializing in the education of children with disabilities. Publishers of special education literature *(Journal of Childhood Communication Disorders)*. Write or call for information packet/catalog of products and services.

Cure Autism Now (CAN)
5225 Wilshire Blvd, Suite 226
Los Angeles, CA 90036
(213) 549-0500/(213) 549-0547 FAX
Portia Iversen, Director. An organization founded by parents who are dedicated to finding effective biological treatments and a cure for autism. CAN'S mission is to fund medical research with direct clinical applications in the field of autism. CAN'S Scientific Work Group is made up of top researchers and clinicians, many of whom are parents of children with autism. CAN believes that it is the parents who will mobilize the scientific and medical communitie into action.

Developmental Delay Registry
4401 EastWest Hwy, Suite 207
Bethesda, MD 20814
(301)652-2263/(301) 652-9133 FAX
www.devdelay.org
Patricia Lemer, Director. National registry of children with developmental delays. Conducts research designed to determine if there are ways to prevent developmental delays and help those affected. Offers workshops and seminars. Publishes membership networking directory.

Different Roads to Learning

12 West 18th St, Suite 3E
New York, NY 10011
(800) 853-1057/(800) 317-1997 FAX
Julie Azuma, President. A catalogue offering skillbuilding toys and playthings focusing on the areas of speech, language, as well as cognitive and fine motor skills.

Epilepsy Foundation of America

4351 Garden City Dr
Landover, MD 20785-2267
(800) 332-1000
Provides information, referrals, and answers basic questions concerning epilepsy. Offers membership and other services including a newsletter.

Facilitated Communication Institute

Syracuse University
370 Huntington Hall
Syracuse, NY 13244-2340
(315) 443-9657
Established to further training, public education, and awareness regarding facilitated communication. Maintains a resource network of persons involved in facilitated communication.

Future Horizons

720 N Fielder
Arlington, TX 76012
(800) 489-0727
Wayne Gilpin, President. Publishes and sells many excellent books and materials specifically on autism as well as ASA conference proceedings. Sponsors autism conferences nationwide. Call or write for product list.

The Geneva Center
250 Davisville Av, Suite 200
Toronto, Ontario, Canada M4S 1H2
(416) 322-7877/(416) 322-5894 FAX
Offers in-service training, assessment and consultation services. Offers many materials on autism. Call or write for information.

Groden Center
86 Mount Hope Av
Providence, RI 02906
(401) 274-6310
Offers information on relaxation techniques for people with autism. Sells books and videos.

Indiana Resource Center for Autism (IRCA)
The Institute for the Study of Developmental Disabilities
2853 E 10th St
Bloomington, IN 47408-2601
(812) 855-6508
Offers many excellent materials concerning autism: booklets,videos, teaching modules. Write or call for free information list.

Journal of Autism and Developmental Disorders
Plenum Publishing Corporation
233 Spring St
New York, NY 10013
(212) 620-8000
Journal focusing on current, professional research on autism.

Locutour Media
1130 Grove St, Suite 300
San Luis Obispo, CA 93401
(800) 777-3166/(805) 543-6665 FAX
Marna Scarry-Larkin, Director. Offers cognitive rehabilitation

CD-ROM technology and other computer software for developing language skills and cognitive retraining.

Miller Educational Tools, Inc.

PO Box 4483
Ft. Lauderdale, FL 33338
(954) 566-6175/(954) 566-7588
Sally Miller, Founder. Offers POCKETS™, an educational tool designed to assist students in developing and practicing the skills involved in organizing information.

More Able Autistic People (MAAP)

PO Box 524
Crown Point, IN 46307
Publishes quarterly newsletter for parents. Sells information packet, "Tips for Teachers," and a parents' handbook.

National Alliance for the Mentally Ill (NAMI)

200 N Glebe, Suite 1015
Arlington, VA 22203
(703) 524-7600/(800) 950-6264
A grass-roots, self-help, support and advocacy organization for families and friends of people of all ages with neurobiological disorders. More than 1,000 affiliates nationwide.

National Fragile X Foundation

1441 York St, Suite 303
Denver, CO 80206
(303) 333-6155/(800) 688-8765
Disseminates research and information on Fragile X Syndrome. Promotes education and awareness of Fragile X. Membership is $40.

National IEP Advocates (NARDA)
PO Box 16111
Sugar Land, Texas 77496-6111
(218) 265-1506
Louis Geigerman, President. NARDA is a fee-based advocacy service that is dedicated to obtaining the appropriate educational services for children with special needs.

National Information Center for Children and Youth With Disabilities (NICHY)
PO Box 1492
Washington, DC 20013
(202) 884-8200/(800) 695-0285
Publishes *NICHY News Digest* (free subscription within US). Provides free information on autism and other disabilities. Can also help in locating educational programs and services for children with disabilities.

Pro-Ed
8700 Shoal Creek Blvd
Austin, TX 78757
(512) 451-3246
Publishes quarterly journal, *Focus on Autism and Other Developmental Disabilities*. Also offers an extensive catalogue of educational materials.

Special Kids Company
PO Box 462
Muskego, WI 53150
(800) KIDS-153
John and Lori Sprecher, Owners. Special Kids offers a large variety of "learning videos" for children with special needs.

Stages Learning Materials
PO Box 27
Chico, CA 95927-0027
(888) 501-8880/(916) 892-9158 FAX
Angela Nelson, Owner. Offers a complete set of flash-cards, featuring shapes, colors, and other objects. The flashcards are designed to teach a variety of fundamental language skills to children with speech and language de-lays or developmental disorders. Free color catalogue available.

Vaccine Information Center
512 West Maple Av, Suite 206
Vienna, VA 22180
(703) 938-0342/(800) 909-SHOT
Provides information on vaccines as well as referrals to physicians and attorneys. Publishes a newsletter, *The Vaccine Reaction*.

Volunteers for Autism Foundation
PO Box 406
South River, NJ 08882
Frank Pasalano, Director. Nonprofit organization founded to provide information, referrals, support, and fund-raising assistance to families of children with autism.

INTERNET URL ADDRESSES

http://www.autism.org/ **Center for the Study of Autism**

http://www.sait.org **Society for Auditory Integration Training**

http://web.syr.edu/~jmwobus/autism/
Autism Resources

http://pages.prodigy.com/dporcari/recovery_zone.html
Information Relating to Lovaas Method

http://fohnix.metronet.com/~thearc/welcome.html
The Arc's Home Page

http://nodulus.extern.ucsd.edu/ **Autism and Brain Development Research Laboratory**

http://www.panix.com/~donwiss/reichelt.html
Collected Net Writings from Dr. Reichelt

http://www.autismNDI.com **Gluten and Casein Free Diet**

http://wonder.mit.edu/ok/ **Our Kids**

http://homepage.seas.upenn.edu/~mengwong/add
Attention Deficit Disorder

bit.listserv.autism **A Newsgroup concerning autism**

http://www.naar.org
National Alliance for Autism Research

http://www.canfoundation.org
Cure Autism Now Foundation

http://www.autism.com/shaw-yeast
Dr. William Shaw. Information on anti-yeast therapy.

http://www.autism.com/ari **Autism Research Institute**

http://www.autism-society.org **Autism Society of America**

http://osiris.sunderland.ac.uk/autism/durham95.html **Dr. Paul Shattock**

http://www.secretin.com **Information on secretin.**

Index

A

B

C

O

P

Notes

Order Form

Help get the information out!

Order the Autism Treatment Guide for:

- ■ A friend
- ■ A doctor
- ■ A teacher
- ■ A library

- -

Please send me _____copies at $12.95 each, plus $2.00 per book shipping and handling in U.S. ($3.50 outside U.S.)

Please print clearly

Name_____

Address _____

City/State/Zip _____

Send check and order form to:

 Four Leaf Press
P.O. Box 23502
Eugene, OR 97402